"Everything's got to end sometime. Otherwise
nothing would ever get started."

The Doctor

(C) Marc W Ford MBA, Your Best Kept Business
ISBN 978-0-244-79551-1

4

# Introduction

For Jemma.

I began writing this in November 2018. I did a 20 minute presentation to a networking group and thought I could do something about business and Dr Who the day after Jodie Whittaker became the first female Doctor in the shows history.

Nothing like being on trend.

24hrs later I ended up doing the same presentation again for a different audience and there was a chap that came up to me afterwards and had a little word with me. His name is Karl. He's a website designer. Also a bit of a self confessed geek, though not about Dr Who.

He suggested I turn the presentation into a 12 part podcast series. Partly because he thought it would be quite cool and probably because I was boring myself with the podcast. I thought about it and thought, 'Why not?'. It'll make it fun.

As I sat and wrote the first podcast, my best friend Jemma, walked into the room and with her usual matter-of-factness (if that was ever a word), said, "Wow, thats the first chapter of your next book."

And so here it is.

Business lessons from Dr Who.

I've spent a while putting this one together and perhaps not everything fits together as coherently as some writers may have done, but as a geek who likes chaos, tough. I'll move forwards, backwards, sideways and upside down in time and references, just like the TARDIS would. I will probably come across as a nerd and truly I don't care.

But I've finished this volume, (there will be one about 'New Who' at some point), and as I sit and write this I wish I had my own TARDIS.

Me and Jemma are no longer together and like many things in life, you are filled with regrets and if I could go back, I would. She was my conscious when I needed it and my muse when I least expected it. If I had ever been lucky enough to play the Doctor, (like I wanted to when I was a kid), she would have been my perfect Sarah-Jane Smith. And it's because of her that this book sees the light of day...


Rose: "I love you..."
The Doctor: "Quite right too...And if it's my last chance to say it..."

(The Doctor fades away...)

## The First Doctor

Doctor Who first appeared on BBC Television on Saturday, 23 November 1963. It was to be a regular weekly programme, with each episode at twenty-five minutes of transmission length. Discussions and plans for the programme had been in progress for the year leading up to it's first episode. The then Head of Drama, Sydney Newman, was mainly responsible for developing the programme, with the first format document for the series being written by Newman along with the head of the script department Donald Wilson and a staff writer, C.E. Webber.

The general premise of the show was that it should appeal to a family audience as an educational programme and using time travel as a means to explore scientific ideas and famous moments in history. But before we talk about the first episode, let's talk about the first business lesson that we could and should all learn from, just by it existing.

Head of Drama, Sydney Newman was brought in to do something a 'little different' with the drama programming. Poached from commercial station ITV, he was a Canadian that was responsible for other hit TV shows such as the Avengers, (the TV show and not the superhero movies), and Armchair Theatre, a staple of British television. He was also seen as an antidote to the stuffy, relatively unproductive, stiff upper-lipped BBC executives that were already in situ, just 'being very British' and serving up very 'straight' Drama. What do I exactly mean by that?

Well at this time in TV history, there were a lot of drama's on the BBC that were essentially well written plays but televised. Historical drama's were the norm and were served up on a regular basis. The Radio Times, the UK's TV scheduling magazine, were full of them. And if you think about it, these would be a 'massive turn off' for the younger audience, unless they liked Shakespeare, had a penchant for plays based in Rome or loved a good old confusing plot based in Victorian London somewhere.

Newman recognised that the BBC had a problem in their TV schedule at the weekend. There was a twenty-five minute slot between the sports programme 'Grandstand' and the 'teeny bopper' magnet that was 'Juke Box Jury' where ratings effectively 'fell off a cliff', only to climb again when the pop music started. Traditional TV drama's just didn't work in that slot, no matter what was out there. There had to be a way to keep the audience engaged and on the station.

And this is where the first business lesson appears, just like a Tardis materialising.

As business owners, we are all problems solvers. Broken down in to it's simplest form, a business is a solution to a customers problem. It doesn't matter what business you are in. You solve someone's problem. Even if they don't realise they actually have a problem.

You could be a business coach, that helps put business owners who are in chaos, in order, and get them making money. You could be a shop owner that provides a one-stop shop for customers to buy all their basic needs. You could even be an undertaker that helps people get rid of a dead relative and puts them in the ground with all the pomp and ceremony that they deserve, without the family digging the hole and dealing with any more unpleasantness. Some are necessary problems that need solving. Some problems are more 'first world' problems. And some are necessary evil problems…you know the ones? The ones that solicitors, estate agents and accountants perform.

Newman looked at his customers problem, in this case the BBC, and began to devise a plan. They didn't 'know' they had a problem although the data that was available at that time, made it fairly obvious. The biggest KPI, (Key Performance Indicator), in TV are the ratings numbers and 'viewer share'. It was a bit of genius if I'm honest, and the next bit I write will show you how 'obvious' the problem was.

Kids and teenagers love sport. As they do now. Dad's loved sport. As many of them do now. Kids and teenagers loved music. Even more so then. They didn't have Spotify, iTunes,Virgin Records, Our Price or even Top of The Pops yet. BBC Radio 1 was four years off it's first broadcast and so there was a massive audience for the music from that TV show alone.

He set about designing and creating a show that would be fun, entertaining, and educational to that family market. There has been a lot said over the last 50-odd years that Dr Who, was a show for kids. I've always questioned that. It's storylines, it's values, it's basic core components were always geared more to a family audience rather than child specific. But that is a whole new book, written by someone with a lot of time on their hands and probably a Doctorate in something. Newman sat down and wrote the original treatment for the show. And that show came in the form of Dr Who, a 25 minute weekly serial drama. It was designed to be a show about a man who traveled through time in his 'ship' visiting places and times of interest. He was to be the older professor type character, probably because back in the 60's we had more respect for teachers and what they did for society. Try getting kids to watch an educational programme like this now, with that premise and it would be very unlikely to ever get off the ground, let alone a second series.

The second lesson that's in this story is something, that for whatever reason, we really haven't learned much from in 55 years. A shame if I'm honest. But we are starting to get there.

This lesson comes in the shape of Newman appointing a female producer and leader of this project in the form of Verity Lambert. A decisive and brave move that caused more than a few tidal waves to those in the BBC. It was a 'man's world' in the 60's and so trying to get anything done by a woman in amongst the structure that was the BBC, was like pushing a rock, up hill, all day, every day. Looking back at the troubles this caused leading up to the first episode, it was amazing it ever aired. But not only was Newman 'diverse' in his choice of producer,

Lambert was just as 'diverse' in her choice of director for the first episodes. Again breaking down a few barriers for it's place in time.

Waris Hussein was a British Indian, born in Lucknow, Uttar Pradesh. And so the team entrusted to brining the first set of episodes together were as diverse as they could be working within a 1960's publicly owned corporation. A Canadian, a woman and someone from an ethnic minority background. Who'd have thought that we still struggle with that crap now, some 55 years later? Bizarre.

So to encapsulate the first two lessons, in one word, that word would be 'Opportunity'. An opportunity presented itself in a 25 minute slot that wasn't being looked after properly, but was a problem dying to be solved. An opportunity to 'break a few barriers' in a heavily male, white, very British corporation presented itself by introducing a female producer and a director of ethnic decent. Nobody ever did anything of worth by playing by the usual rules. Look through history. Great business leaders have often bent, changed or turned the rules of the game on their heads, to become the success we recognise today.

With the leadership team set, the run up to filming the first episode was at best, 'troublesome'. Actually it sounded like a very hard road, just to get one episode made. Various articles, stories and documentaries show that no-one at the corporation took the 'problem' of those 25 minutes very seriously. From set designs not being designed, to set building not being completed on time; being forced to use a knackered old studio where the sprinkler system would go off if it got too hot from the studio lights; scripts not being written or ready; to actually finding an actor to play the lead role. These were just a few of the problems the team faced. Yet the vision and goal were always there. Solve the problem of those 25 minutes.

Eventually they hired actor William Hartnell. A seasoned and somewhat veteran character actor, he took the role on, with a provisor that it it wouldn't type cast him or shackle him with work. Little did he know that it was a role that would define his work and arguably, a role for who he would still be remembered above all others. 55 years later we Dr Who fans still talk about him and his work on the series, where it is looked upon with fondness and huge gratefulness. If it wasn't for him, I wouldn't be writing this.

So let's time travel forward a little to the recording of the first pilot.

It was crap. Utterly awful.

People forgetting their lines, bumping into stuff and cameras bumping into one another. It was never aired. Newman, as I'm led to believe, was the only man to see it and called the producer and director to a meeting. This is where the third lesson lies. Test whatever you do first before you launch it.

If it had been aired, I probably wouldn't be talking to you about it right now. Newman wrote a ream of notes and gave them to the producer and director, giving them a chance to put things right at the expense of the Corporation itself. To effectively bin an episode back in the sixties was almost like pouring a sackful of cash down the drain. It was unheard of. But Newman realised that the effect of not getting it right would cost them more money in the long run. Sets, actors and contracts would cost an even bigger fortune to mothball. Something to always think about when developing your own ideas and products. There comes a point in time, where there is no point of return and to 'bin' something completely, may cost you more than going through with the idea or concept.

They remade the pilot, which doubled for the first episode. It launched on Saturday November 23rd 1963.

To shocking ratings.

It was the day after American President, John F Kennedy had been assassinated and as a nation, along with power blackouts across the country, we weren't particularly interested in sport or Juke Box Jury. We were watching news reports and listening to radio updates. The BBC were doing what it was good at. News.

They were busy doing what they had always done and didn't waste their time with promoting a first episode of a time-travelling family drama. Knowing and being certain that he had a hit on his hands, Newman convinced his bosses, the stuffed suits above him, to allow him to repeat the first episode, right before the second episode, one week later. It was a success. The first series containing 42 episodes aired to an average of 8 million people over a 10 month period.

Another lesson showing itself here, is that if you wait for the 'perfect time' to do something, it will never happen. Sometimes you have to make the time. Be bold and effective in when you do something, no matter how ready you really feel. Effectively this programme was launched three times. It's original unaired episode. It's aired episode. And its repeated episode. Lessons learned each time and done better the next. The passion, vision and drive to see the job done, was like nothing the BBC had experienced before. And 55 years later we should thank the team for that. It would have been far easier, for everyone probably, just to let it 'happen'.

I also want to touch on something else that as I was writing this, popped into my head, and may come out as a mini rant. I apologise if it does, but I think it needs to be said. (And to give you a flavour of what else is in this book, you might find me doing it again at various points.)

The first series contained 42 episodes. 42 episodes!

Nowadays that is almost unheard of. But before any of you 'TV buffs' say weekly shows like Coronation Street or Eastenders broadcast more, I want to throw this back at you. The core cast of Dr Who were effectively 4 people. 4 people! The Doctor, his grand-daughter, and two teachers. Latterly it went down to 3 members of core cast. Add to that guest cast, extra's, new sets, new stories, new monsters and new technical challenges virtually on a weekly basis. Long running drama's nowadays have casts well into double figures with shorter scenes and sets permanently in one place. Plus the additional benefit of CGI, data transferring, off site editing, being able to film for however long they want and when they want. TV actors and production teams, have never had it so good! That was hard work.

Dr Who's success was not just down to it's innovation in the drama genre at that particular time. In my opinion, it's success rested just as heavily with the amount of sheer hard work and the graft that went into the project by the team behind the scenes. As we currently sit here in 2018, we are surrounded by a stack of people, coaches and writers that tell you to close your eyes, dream a dream and it will all come true, because you want it to.

## STOP IT! STOP IT NOW!

Here is some genuine business reality. 'Everyone's', 'Anyones' and 'Someone's' success is always down to the hard work put in to climb the steps to get to that success. It works hand in hand with a vision or goal. If it really means something to you, it will move you forward towards it, but putting the time and effort into something will actually make it 'happen'. Otherwise you'd be dreaming of winning a huge sum on the lottery but you never play the lottery. So how the hell do you expect to get there?

It means getting up and doing what you need to do, every single day, to get to where you need to be, even if you don't feel like it. Working longer and harder than others. Proving people wrong. Making mistakes, learning from them and continually pushing yourself to achieve that goal or dream. There are no shortcuts. It's simple. The more you do, the smarter you get. The smarter you get, the better you get. The better you are, the sweeter the end result. These guys in November 1963 through to September 1964 worked day and night. Rehearsed, wrote, rewrote, created, built, changed, adapted, learned and produced an end result for nearly a year to attract the audience and the following they wanted. It was through that hard work that they became a national sensation.

It was true that they had their bit of luck. But the harder you work, the luckier you get. That's a fact. And it could then be considered not 'as lucky' as you'd think. People started queuing up to write scripts for Dr Who. People let their 'availability' be known. The luck, or a massive step to success, however you look at it, boiled down to someone asking a writer to create a villain for a story. And boy, did they create one of the most well known, feared and hide behind your sofa kind of villains that the world has ever seen!

Writer Terry Nation gave us the Daleks. From the very first episode that they appeared in, with the iconic 'assistant scream' whilst looking at a sink plunger at the end of the episode, children up and down the nation were hooked. And if truth be told, so were the parents. It had become family viewing. Dr Who had given us something to unite behind or appreciate, however you look at it. It gave birth to Dalek-mania. And that was a real thing by the way.

Here my friends is the next lesson. Every business should have 'a cause', 'a reason' or a 'why' to for customers to get behind. In the last decade, individuals have told businesses and the people that run them that they need as many eyes on them as possible, no matter what the cost. Get as many 'likes' on your page. As many followers as you can, buy them if you must because it means something. Not sure what, but it means something. The bigger your likes, loves and retweets you get, it shows other people that you're very important. Wrong. Utter rubbish.

There is one truth that no matter what flash marketers say, has been proven over and over and over again. People buy from people. It doesn't matter wether that's as an individual or as part of the ethos of a business, people will always buy from people. A businesses ethos comes from someone. Somewhere. And that's what people buy into. I'm a massive fan of Simon Sinek's 'Golden Circles' video and his book 'Find Your Why'. He breaks the 'magic sauce' of success down in to the three components, of 'What a business does', 'How a business does it' and 'Why a business does it at all'. Every business knows what they do. Most businesses know how they do it. Very few know why they do it. The successful ones? They know why the do it. A purpose, a cause, a reason why and they learn to communicate it through their marketing and their work.

Whilst we're talking about these things on a purely entertainment basis, they gave people a genuine reason 'why' they should watch Dr Who. They gave them a villain that scared the crap out of children up and down the country. It bought families together. It played on a 1960's public fear of war, technology, the unknown and a fear of the future. (You need to remember, that it hadn't even been 20 years, since World War 2.) The BBC found themselves in a position that they didn't need to advertise Dr Who. It was being done by word of mouth. If you'd missed it on Saturday night and because it was the talk of the playground on a Monday morning, you made sure you saw it the following week. No videos or hard-drive boxes then. It was always broadcast on a Saturday tea-time, week in, week out. Dependable. Did what it always did. Great quality for it's time in entertainment and in many peoples eyes, was way ahead of it's time.

Lying within the programme itself, the Daleks taught us another business lesson. If the Daleks were the Doctors true nemesis, then your competitors should be considered yours. The Daleks, did not care about your feelings, your environment, your quality of life, your bills, your bank balance or your standing in the community. They EXTERMINATED you.

Simple. Your competitors don't care about you. Never have and never will. They want to EXTERMINATE you. FACT.

They are taking your ideal customers and clients away from you. They are destroying your capacity to earn and to grow. The Doctor however, never, ever used guns or heavy artillery to beat his nemesis. He just used his guile, wit, intelligence and experience to outsmart them. They all have. All 13 Doctors have done that. It's a main stay of the characters personality and through various decades it would be have been 'trendy' to use that heavy type of shortcut to defeat an enemy. (Yes, Dr Who fans, he did have U.N.I.T. But lets be fair, they were pretty bloody useless whenever they used a gun, grenade or a tank!) It would have only been a short term victory and a victory at a personal cost to the main character. A quick fix. The same in business.

There is nothing to be proud of if you 'crush' your competition by heavy discounting, heavy marketing and bullying tactics. If you think you should do these things I offer you a word of warning - there is always someone better and a bigger bully than you around the corner. There is always a cost either financially or to a reputation. It's a short term tactic, that whilst it does work, it only lasts as long as your customers remain uneducated. As soon as they work out there is another way, a better way, a smarter way, they begin to follow those people and businesses. Because it's what they want, and what they believe in. What do you want to be remembered as? An elite type of brand, or a heavy discounter operating out of the back of a van? These types of tactics define businesses. Just look at all the furniture, beds and carpet places that promote heavy discounting, week after week, after week.

Does the biggest furniture business and brand on the planet, 'IKEA', use those same tactics?

No. Not at all. And yet in the continual up and down market that is retail, they are still growing and the discounters are looking at rescue packages and closing stores down.

The same goes for high street fashion retailer, Primark. As I write this they have just opened their largest ever store which has taken over an actual shopping centre, based on five floors, with nearly 1,000 staff members in a time when retailers are contracting rather than growing. Concerns about the ethics of their products aside, they give the customer exactly what they want, have little to no online presence, don't heavily market and are growing at a rate that their competition are just looking on with their mouths wide open.

So use your guile, your experience, your uniqueness, your wit and your smartness to attract your ideal customers and clients. Because they'll stick with you. They'll run through walls for you. They'll support you in good times and bad...just like the Doctors companions and core fandom always have done.

Austin Kleon, author of the book, 'Show Your Work' says, "You want hearts, not eyeballs." It's true. I very rarely see an Apple advert. But here I am writing this on an iPhone, an iPad and iMac. I fell in love with the simplicity of the whole thing. The simplicity of the whole brand. The ease of use and the effect that it has had on my working life and my career. They've made stuff easy for me. They've made me more productive. And that has my heart.

This was also a lesson on the right time to 'cash-in' on the stratospheric reactions that the public had to the Daleks. Way before George Lucas came up with his plastic toys, the BBC had encouraged companies to make toys, books, games, soap, bubble bath and clothes of Dr Who and the Daleks. It even spun off into two feature length movies seen in cinemas the world over. Dr Who and the Daleks, starring Peter Cushing as the Doctor was made in 1965, in Hartnell's second year. And Daleks Invasion Earth 2150AD was made in Hartnell's last year, again starring Cushing, but was received poorly at the Box Office. Effectively they were bigger budgeted and longer episodes of the TV show. Where George Lucas 'won' was keeping hold of the rights to things. Something the BBC has gotten round to eventually, but imagine how much more it could have made the Corporation back then. I'll touch more on this in a later book, (probably around Doctor number 9), because they almost got that formula right!

The next lesson, in all it's glory, that will be forever associated with the first Doctor is a lesson of reimagining and building something bigger than just one person when it's the right time to move in a different direction. In his last series between 1965 and July 1966, Hartnell began showing increasing signs of being unwell. He was coping with arteriosclerosis, which had began to affect his ability to learn lines. Producer Verity Lambert had decided to move on to pastures new and Hartnell, well known for being 'difficult' to work with at the best of the times, was struggling to get on with the new production team. The pressure was there for everyone to see. This could have been the end for the show. How could it go on without it's lead man? And what would happen to the now nearly 10 million viewers it had on a weekly basis?

Newman had the answer. The Doctor is an alien. So what's stopping the character from 'renewing' his body and shape if he got old, ill or died?

This became what's known as 'regeneration' and has become a staple, a 'must see' TV moment throughout the shows history for the public to see what the new person looks like and how different they are to the previous one. It gave the show a chance to have a different tone, different direction, different stories and a fresh impetus. It was genius.

It suddenly made this show about a man in an old Police Box travelling through time and space into a different show about a different man in an old Police Box travelling through time and space. It had the same core values. The same problems needed solving. The same customers, and some new ones needed entertaining on a Saturday tea-time. And this was the way to do it. Change the leader. Change the image. Become more modern. Keep up with changing times. Offer the customers an alternative to what you'd always been, and what you've always done.

The lesson was simple. If it's right to change, change. Even if that means you have to change your success team or change your people within your leadership team. It maybe considered selfish, but your legacy will be viewed very differently if you choose not to change.

A business or person that isn't growing is failing or dying according to Tony Robbins. I'd agree. So personal and business growth should become a normal path to follow, but how you choose to follow that path may involve decisions that are necessary for that growth to continue. It maybe painful, but not confronting those decisions will become even more painful given time. Change is inevitable in business, it's just how you handle it that can make a big difference to you and your business.

Finally, on a Saturday tea-time in July 1966, Hartnell fell to floor as the First Doctor. His cape positioned perfectly. Looking like one of those chalk drawings around a dead body on a detective show. The picture of a moist brow in black and white. And with basic TV trickery, the image had turned into a man named Patrick Troughton. There, on their TV for children everywhere, there was a bloke who wasn't the

Doctor. For TV executives, on that same TV, was a gamble and a journey into the unknown.

So a quick recap of the business lesson from the First Doctor...

1.  **Opportunity.** See a problem and solve it. Choose the team that suits you and not the norm. To make the most of that opportunity, sometimes, just sometimes, you have to break a few barriers down and bend a few rules to solve the problem that lays before your customers and clients. The really brave, take the game and turn it on it's head along with the rules.
2.  **Test stuff** before you launch anything. Websites, courses, presentations, speeches, products and services. In most walks of life you only get one opportunity to impress. React to the feedback and sort what's wrong. Quickly. Don't test stuff and you'll be spoken about in the wrong way.
3.  **Graft**. It takes real graft, not just from you, but everyone in your success team or leadership team to make your vision and goals happen. It's great to have a clear mental image of where you're going, but unless you put in the time and effort, that's all they'll ever be. Mental images.
4.  **Give people a reason 'why'** they should get behind you. Why should they follow you? Customer and clients will go through brick walls to support you if they believe in what you're doing as a business. Grab peoples hearts, rather than

concentrating on getting lots and lots of eyes on you.

5. **View your competitors as a nemesis**. Look at them. Learn from them. Be better than them. Keep learning. And use longer term tactics to be better and grow your business. Quick fixes that work, become addictive. Too addictive and similar to that of drugs. You'll look for the next quick fix. It will be at a cost to you and your business financially and your reputation. Eventually quick fixes lead to collapses. A bit like a drug.

6. **Recognise the time for change and don't be afraid of it**. Change can be good. It puts wind back in your sails and can take you to new heights you've only dreamt of. It comes with risk, but without risk there will never be any gains. Refuse to change, you'll never grow. Don't grow and it becomes harder work to even stand still. Listen to your customers. They'll tell you when you need to change. Don't let the pressure build. Be decisive. Have a different strategy. Devise another plan.

# The Second Doctor

You never want to be the person to follow 'that guy' do you? You know the one.

The 'David Moyes guy'. He followed Sir Alex Ferguson after he had retired from football management at Manchester United. The Gordon Brown after Tony Blair quit as Prime Minister. The Adam Lambert after Freddie Mercury passed away as Queen's frontman. Those types of people.

It never usually ends well. But someone has to do it.

And because of that you always worry about how people are going to accept change. One of the things I've learned in my 40-odd years alive on this tiny little planet, is that we all cope with change really well. And actually we cope far better than we give ourselves credit for. It was 'change' that was big gamble for the BBC and Dr Who in 1966. With a new production team and it's lead actor too ill to carry the show, Sydney Newman came up with an idea that would carry it through to the present day. The transformation into the Second Doctor (originally referred to as a "renewal"), a figure who was the same 'essential' character as the first but with a very different persona, was a turning point in the evolution of the series, and eventually became a critical element of the series' longevity.

The First Doctor had grown progressively weaker in his last story whilst battling with another foe that kids talked about every week. The Cybermen. It was art imitating real life. Hartnell was becoming increasingly frail, but at the end of the story, the Doctor returned to his ship, the TARDIS, and collapsed. His body renewed itself and turned into the body of Patrick Troughton.

Initially, the relationship between the Second Doctor and his predecessor was unclear. In his first story, the Doctor referred to his predecessor in the third person as if he were a completely different person. His companions Ben and Polly are at first unsure how to treat him and it is only when a Dalek recognises him that they accept that he is the Doctor. And that's how the second Doctor launched himself into history. He'd come with new titles and with his pesky little face at the start of the episode. The music had stayed the same, it gave comfort to the viewers. But the changes were there for everyone to see.

The Radio Times was inundated with letters from people saying they 'loved the new Doctor', to those that thought Troughton had reduced the character down to that of a 'clowning tramp'. The latter stuck, and this Doctor was often referred to as the 'Cosmic Hobo', and in the same breath has been named as THE influence on how other actors have played the part.

Hartnell gave his blessing to Troughton. Sir Alex Ferguson gave his blessing to David Moyes. Tony Blair begrudgingly gave his blessing to Gordon Brown. Perhaps a kiss of death?

Newman saw the make-up and costume tests, but demanded that he was turned into a 'Cosmic Hobo'. Between him and the new producer his casting was to make him significantly different to the previous incarnation. The original idea had been to recast the role, but for someone similar to play the exact same role. That would never have worked, (as it didn't in the 1980's when another actor was recast as the First

Doctor), and the public weren't to be treated that stupidly.

The old Doctor had been the dapper, well dressed, Victorian style gentleman. This Doctor was wearing oversized checked trousers held up by comedy braces with an un-ironed crumpled shirt, A bow tie around a collar that was always asquif.

His first episodes were to show this Doctor as aloof, slightly self absorbed and not spending any time explaining his actions; much to the frustration of his companions and some of the audience.

But his child like behaviour was just a 'front' put on as the stories unfolded and the enemies plots grew clear. Then the hardened, wise, precise side of the character came out. It was at this point we all knew it was the exact same character that we had always known and many had grown up with.

It was Troughton that took on the responsibility of showing the audience that the show could go on with a different leader actor, and in part character, but with exactly the same core concepts of drama, education and fun.

However public opinion was divided. Some of the letters written to the BBC and the Radio Times had comments such as, "...he didn't seem right somehow" and "Once a brilliant but eccentric scientist, he now comes over as a half-witted clown." Responses to change back in the past are just the same as they are now. Except now we have social media.

Here's a business lesson from the second Doctor. When someone new steps in to lead a business or brand, there are bound to be people who disapprove. Unless you've done something really bad in a past life, there are as many people within an organisation or outside it, that are just as willing to give you a chance to prove yourself.

The 'business' of Dr Who was built upon the shoulders of one man. Hartnell. His shoulders 'carried' the franchise for 3 years. In most people's eyes, he started it. He WAS Dr Who. It's unthinkable that anyone else could be him. But for the reasons that I've touched on, for the programme to continue, it had to happen. A successors role is far more difficult than a creators role.

A great example of how things could potentially go wrong is the story of Apple. Steve Jobs and Steve Wozniak created and built Apple. They added John Sculley to the board of Directors. But it became apparent that the 'vision' for Apple of Jobs and Sculley were vastly different. In June 1985, the board of directors sided with Sculley and Jobs was stripped of all duties. Jobs, while taking the position of Chairman of the firm, had no influence over Apple's direction and subsequently resigned. Sculley reorganised the company, unifying sales and marketing in one division and product operations and development in another. In a show of defiance at being set aside by Apple Computer, Jobs sold all but one of his 6.5 million shares in the company for $70 million.

However Sculley got it wrong. It could be argued that because he hadn't walked the successful steps to creating the Apple brand, that when the pressure was on, and competition became fierce, he was unable to move the company back up those same steps. On July 9, 1997, Jobs was asked to step in as the interim CEO of Apple to begin a critical restructuring of the company's product line. He would eventually become CEO and served in that position until August 2011. On August 24, 2011 Steve Jobs resigned his position as chief executive officer of Apple before his long battle with pancreatic cancer took his life on October 5, 2011. The rest they say is history. And I'm guessing you didn't expect that story about Apple? Tim Cook's story with Apple is still continuing.

Some would say that Job's ran a big danger to his career by returning to the business he built and he is probably one of the few people in business that could have made it work. But the reason I told you this story, is that it demonstrates how hard it is to be the person that follows 'the guy'. Safe to say that Tim Cook is doing a good job in running a world class business now. History in business can teach us so many things.

Failure teaches just as much as success.

So back to Troughton. The show had to keep up with it's audience and keep relevant...something many businesses fail to do. Some of the audience would be encountering it for the first time, and it makes sense that the show needed to change with the actor. The production teams first decision was to abolish all 'pure historical' stories. The lure of pure science fiction and exotic aliens were too big.

The format of the show began to change and for this Doctor they found a winning formula. Partly because of financial reasons and partly for time constraints, the formula for most of Troughton's era was the 'Base Under Siege' formula. They walk in; Base is under siege from villains; they save the day from where they are. Simple right?

From a business perspective this would constitute a brave move. Some would say foolish. But in retrospect, they 'got away' with it. When a business has a 'winning formula', it seems ridiculous to change it. But they did.

It only seems ridiculous until you swap it for a better one. In business, financial reasons to change things are always a pressure, but there are others too. In this case, and as many companies do, the BBC wanted more for the same, if not less. (This would be something that would bite the show on it's ass in the 1980's but we'll cover that later.) Some dress this up as productivity, others dress this up as progress. The best example of someone taking something and reformulating things for the better would be Amazon and it's approach to retail.

However, I'd say that like Amazon, most successful businesses and 'game changers' in industry don't just trip over successful formula's. They look at something relatively basic, but hugely powerful. I call it S.T.E.P. (Some of you may know it is as P.E.S.T. but I prefer to put it in order of ease of things you can influence.)

So S stands for 'Social', T stands for 'Technological', E stands for 'Environmental' and P stands for 'Political'. As well as using this as a gauge of where the world is today, I find this hugely useful when looking at what things I can incorporate IN TO my business, rather than just what AFFECTS my business. Being ahead of a wave rather than chasing it or being in amongst it is always favourable in business. So being able to change or 'tinker' with a winning formula before you need to do it, means you are writing your own rules. BUT...and it's a big but...the core, the heart, the soul, the vision or the aim has to remain the centre of any formulaic change in your business.

How will it effect the customer?
Does it make things better for your customers?
Does it make their lives easier?
Cheaper?
Less stressful?
Will it help them grow?
Will it way-lay their fears?
By changing the formula, are you changing the problem that you solve or creating a new one?

Keeping up with change and reflecting what was really going on in the world came in the shape of a returning foe for Dr Who. One of the main villains in the second Doctors tenure, were the Cybermen. Not as popular as the Daleks, this villain was developed for Hartnell's last story as something even more dark and sinister, even if we kids didn't quite 'get it'.

Throughout the 60's the increase of mind altering drugs both legal and illegal were becoming more of a worry for dehumanising people. Combine that with the fear of major organ transplants which were revolutionising medical health care at the time along with the start of the use of prosthetics, there were some common fears that the writers played upon.

The beauty of this villain was that it was not immediately iconic, but they sort of crept up on you. The second Doctor would meet the Cybermen four times in three years. Each time their design had changed slightly, but with their key features staying the same, so that you knew who they were. They were still the Cybermen, just better every time they came to have a go at ruling the galaxy. I guess you could call the Cybermen as the 'addicted plastic surgery villains' of their time. But you knew that they were the same, emotionless, evil killers they had always been. They just got faster, sleeker and ever so slightly more human like. It played to the fears of the public at the time and that's what made us accept them.

It would also be fair to say that there are many businesses that have played upon the fears of human kind to increase its market share or sales as a whole. Thinking back to the 1980's, not many people did well out of the new epidemic that was 'AIDS' other than the manufacturers of condoms. It shows how the previous lesson of a STEP analysis can truly help you think about what your business can offer by looking at your business through different eyes.

What began to creep into the show during Troughton's tenure were 'jumping-on points' or 'reboots', something of which we see a lot nowadays. New audiences were finding it. New companions began to appear at the start of series so that they would play the part of that non-fan friend, that would ask the questions, only for the Doctor to answer. "What is this place?", "It's the TARDIS, my home.", "The TARDIS?", " It stand for...", yada, yada, yada, etc, etc...

The reason for this is that if you were 10 at the start of Dr Who, you'd be 16 by the end of Troughton's era and things like the opposite sex started entering your head as opposed to skipping, playing football or getting home on a Saturday tea-time to watch a sci-fi drama on a black and white telly with your folks. It was also because of the spread of the television itself. TV was still not an object that every household owned or even rented. So viewing figures, collated as they were back then, were always going to grow because more people had a telly, let alone watched a particular programme. It therefore made sense to having a jumping on point for new viewers.

The same should be said for customers. Many small businesses suffer with this and expect to continue to sell their own product or one service and that's enough. Having a 'jumping on point' means that you can service someone's need despite any difficulties.

Let me explain this in a simple way. When you go into a supermarket, there is usually an 8ft by by 6ft display of Beans. Beans are Beans. So why so many? In this case it helps us show the financial mobility of people either up or down. At the bottom of the list, and probably sold in more units, are the 'everyday value' beans. 20p. Then you can have the own brand beans. 35p. Then you could choose the ones with sausages in. 40p. Then you could choose a Big Brand Bean for 49p. Then a Big Brand with Sausages for 59p. Then a Premium Tin of Beans for 65p. A four pack of premium beans for £2.50 or a six pack for £3.25. I have no idea whether those prices are correct, but it illustrates that at some point in that selection is a 'jumping on point'. Which means you can go up the scale as well down the scale. You win the lottery you can have premium stuff. Lose your job, you can always have the basics.

It was a smart move by the BBC and should be a smart move for you. There are many businesses, especially in retail, that use the ends of certain periods in the year to have a 'store reset'. They do it because they know that due of various reasons and a little of human nature wanting a change, people will be leaving other providers and looking for something different, something new in a different place. Having that jumping on point of a basic offering allows the business to show a true representation of itself in it's simplest form.

The gruelling production schedule....over 130 episodes in a three year period, as well as the fear of being type-cast, led Troughton to hand over the keys to the brand to someone else. The show was in need of another shake-up as it was heading for a new decade, the 1970's, and wanted to keep it's audience engaged. It was a massive clear out. All the regular cast and production team, saw this as an opportunity to move on to pastures new. There was to be a brand new management team put in place.

But during his tenure, it was fair to reflect upon the continued building of the brand. It had been seen by some that it would be difficult task, but the actor and the production staff had done a sterling job. Remember no TV series had re-cast it's leading role and been so blatant about the fact it was 'meant' to be someone different. American shows had recast characters, and the actors playing them had been direct replacements for the previous actors. This was a programme who chose to thrive on it being someone different. During his second incarnation, the Doctor confronted familiar foes such as the Daleks and the Cybermen, as well as new enemies such as the Great Intelligence and the Ice Warriors. It was during this time that he first met the Brigadier, Alistair Gordon Lethbridge-Stewart and became the leader of the British contingent of UNIT, a military organisation tasked to investigate and defend the world from extraterrestrial threats.

The production team balanced old favourites with new characters and foes. Something that business in the current climate struggle to balance. For some reason businesses sit in the 'we have always done it this way' camp or 'let's keep trying to something new and forget our existing customers' camp.

The most successful companies strike a balance. The have a core offering that works. No doubt about it. It works. But they also reach out to their clients and customers and engage with them in relation as to what 'new problems' they can solve. The Dr Who team were doing just that. They were keeping the balance of giving the viewers what they had always wanted and something new. Making it interesting and sexy to like it. They were also using what us geeks call 'fandom' as a sounding board. There are many stories that suggest someone was paid to read lots of stuff, letters, articles and books looking for references to Dr Who and what people would have liked to have seen. This was given to writers and the production team.

Was the second Doctors tenure a success? Well if you look at it from a ratings point of view, perhaps not. Shows peaked at 9million and bottomed at 4million, so it would be fair to say, at best it was hit and miss. But it was a difficult position to be in. Troughton came in as the man to follow the 'guy'. And as discussed before, it's a thankless task. You'd never get the plaudits if it went well, because all the success would have been because of the other guy. If it went badly, it was because you weren't as good as the other guy. Looking back on the era some years later, we'd say it was a success, probably because of the knowledge of the failures that were yet to come. His legacy out lived his life unfortunately. And as a fan, it was sad that people thought of his work so fondly after he had passed. Looking at later incarnations of the Doctor through Sylvester McCoy and Matt Smith, you can tell that they were heavily influenced by Troughton's portrayal. Imitation is the best form of acceptance of success. So nowadays his tenure is viewed as a success.

The Second Doctor's time came to an end when the TARDIS landed in the middle of a war-zone, created by a race of alien warlords who, with the help of another renegade Time Lord the War Chief, progressively kidnapped and brainwashed humans into becoming soldiers for them, hoping to use the ones who survived to conquer the Galaxy. Although the Doctor was able to defeat their plan, he realised he would be unable to return the human subjects to their various original points in Earth's history. He therefore contacted the Time Lords, (thus creating a mythology and telling us his back story), sacrificing his own freedom in the process, and despite an attempt to escape was forced to return to his home planet. He was then put on trial by the Time Lords, for breaking their laws of non-interference. Despite the Doctor's argument that the Time Lords should use their great powers to help others, he was sentenced to exile on 20th century Earth, the Time Lords forcing his regeneration into the Third Doctor in the process. Jamie and Zoe, Troughton's companions, were returned to their own time, with their memories of all but their first encounter with the Doctor wiped and the secret of the TARDIS was also taken from the Doctor.

But that's not all that was taken from the Doctor. So were the 1960's...and black and white.

Here's a quick recap of the Second Doctor

1. **No one wants to be the person who follows 'the guy'**, but inevitably it will happen. There are as many people who want you to succeed as there people who want you to fail. It comes with the territory.
2. **Being that person will divide opinion**. Grow a thick skin. Whilst back in the 60's there were letters to the editor, now we have Social Media. It's just the same but quicker.
3. **When the next generation fails, it's not the end**. There are as many lessons in failure as there are in success. Learn from the failures and move on. If someone is in the wrong position then move them on, or move them downwards. I didn't say this earlier but as I was writing this it struck me. No one has ever woken up and said they wanted to be a manager, or even a business owner. You certainly didn't say it when you were at a school careers day. We actually wake up one morning and find that we are one. We become 'accidental managers' or 'accidental business owners'. It's a life lesson when things don't work, but in most cases it's just not the right fit for the right business...just ask John Sculley.
4. **Look at your business and the world around you in equal measure**. Don't be blinkered. Use the S.T.E.P. Analysis I spoke of earlier. Sociological, Technological, Environmental and Political. Use this with regard to what is affecting

your business and how you can use it to work FOR your business.

5. **Businesses should use emotions in selling and their positioning**. People buy on feelings and if they 'feel' threatened, or loved, or any other deep feeling, they will usually be attracted to you and start a customer/client relationship with you.

6. **Are you cutting your nose off to spite your face?** Have you got 'jumping on' points in your business? Is there a lower end product or service that your customers can join you on or a premium product that the wealthier client would want? Either way, by not just offering a one size all fits all, it will improve your cash flow.

7. **Know when to get out**. If it's too tough or you feel like you're stifled, then it's usually the right time to get out. It really is the only way you should think about it in business. If you hate what you do, it's a chore and you are struggling just to stay still, move on and don't look back. There will always be other opportunities, other things for you to enjoy what you're doing. The only things we regret in life are the things we haven't done. Unless you are a serial killer we never lie on our death bed and say, "I wish I hadn't...", we usually always say, "I wish There is no such thing as a career for life. Just ask all those people who have lost their jobs over the last ten years, including those in the public sector.

## The Third Doctor

Ladies and Gentlemen, welcome to the 1970's. The decade should be looked as a pivot of change. 4 day weeks, 3 day weeks, power shortages. Rubbish being piled high on the streets. Strikes. Awful fashion statements. Star Wars. Colour TV.

It's here that The Third Doctor as portrayed by actor John Pertwee lost his first battle. He lost black and white TV. Progress.

But at the same it was a sign of things to come as this was to be the one of the most turbulent periods in the shows history. There were as many highs as there were lows. And by the end of the decade it certainly would have it's wounds of maturity. So let's jump in with one of the lessons that became very apparent during his tenure as I've mentioned it so early on.

The Third Doctor stories were the first to be broadcast in colour. The early ones were conveniently set on Earth due to cost constraints on the series, because of it's switch to colour.

While previous Doctors' stories had all involved time and space travel, for production reasons, (i.e. cost cutting...which some people call 'keeping an eye on the money'), Pertwee's stories initially depicted the Doctor stranded on Earth in exile, where he worked as a scientific advisor to the international military group UNIT. Within the story, the Third Doctor came into existence as part of a punishment from his own race, the Time Lords, who forced him to regenerate and also disabled his TARDIS. Eventually, this restriction is lifted and the Third Doctor embarks on more traditional time travel and space exploration stories.

If you were to have landed from Mars and been told to watch the episodes of Dr Who with Pertwee, you could be forgiven for thinking its wasn't a show about time or space. The only 'space' element that was consistent is that the planet earth seemed to have moved up in the list of most eligible planets to rule as every Tom, Dick and Alien began arriving to stake their claim. Shops, hospitals, bunkers, warehouses, streets, back alleys, quarries, caves and good old TV studio's were all the settings for the next few years.

This, along with personnel changes and the world changing so rapidly, altered the shape of the series and was a risky evolution at best. It had started it's departure away from it's core 'reason for being'. And as time would go on, it's departure from it's main vision would ultimately, in my opinion lead to it's downfall. But we will come to that later. It's 'reason for being' was very definitely the entertainment, but Sydney Newman, it's creator, had decided it also needed to have an educational meaning. It's now lack of historical stories were going partly un-noticed at the beginning of the 70's, but there was a 'game-changer' on the horizon. The show did try to 'educate', but in a different sense to the original ideas. Stories that reflected adult issues of the time began to slip in. Whilst it was still considered a 'children's show', it was trying to deliver a more meaningful message to the parents that sat with the children to watch on a Saturday tea-time. It also began to use more and more special effects than it had ever done.

Green screens were becoming common practice as the producers wanted to broaden the shows appeal. Some worked. Most didn't. Looking back, some of the special effect have aged very badly, almost making watching some episodes quite embarrassing. They take you out of the story with such a jolt, that you forget what you were thinking before they appeared - everybody should love a good rubber dinosaur.

A lesson here and perhaps a recurring theme would be the fact that moving away from core principles and ideas, will confuse people. There are many businesses who set out to do 'one thing' and then as time progresses they diversify into 'other things'. This leaves the plate of the main core product or service spinning dangerously slowly as time, effort and money are put into 'other things' that the business may well not be known for. If we look at some modern companies, the lessons are there to see. If you look at Microsoft, their vision was to have a computer on everyones desk or home. They succeeded.

However they then started looking into devices such as mp3 players and mobile phones. It hasn't worked so well. Taking a look at it's rival Apple, they became well known for mp3 players such as the iPod. They knew they weren't going to compete in the home or business PC market, because when Steve Jobs walked back in through the doors at the second attempt they had less than 10% of the market. They then added that mp3 functionality to a phone. Why have two devices, when one is easier? Those phones had useful and functional apps, that made our lives slightly more enjoyable or productive everyday. Then they created the iPad, which was now a combination of the mp3 player, a phone and a small laptop computer. All these devices spoke to each other in a simple way. It isn't complicated or needs endless updates and patches. They almost filled in the blanks from the bottom upwards, to the iMac. No-one else got it. Right here is one of the keys to Steve Jobs' success. Apple continued to spin the plates they needed to as people progressed up their 'value chain' of products. They also became 'inclusive' of other software and brand names. Microsoft did not. They've lost a lot of ground by not doing the simple things well or reacting quickly enough. Spinning one plate at a time, and trying to be exclusive. Apple gained the ground and over-took, by spinning all of the plates properly and not leaving their core values behind. They've made our lives easier. Microsoft did that once. Now I'm afraid they don't.

So you can see why it's important to really think on what implications it could have on your business when you want to 'change things' significantly or diversify into other areas of business. It's at this point I'd like to provide some fun and a little bit of balance, because sometimes diversification can happen by accident and have astounding results.

In the UK we have a lovely breakfast cereal called 'Shreddies'. They are lovely little squares of stuff that look like they've been knitted together. In Canada, they weren't as well received and the marketing budget had been pretty much 'spent' to try to make them work. This was until an out-of-work comedian and intern called Hunter Somerville came along and created a sensation in an old product, that led to one of the oddest diversifications. If you can imagine a square, it's not just a square is it? No. Turn it 45 degrees and it's a diamond. And lo, the birth of 'Diamond Shreddies' began. There are videos of 'taste tests' with genuine, real Canadian people who thought that Diamond Shreddies tasted better than ordinary Shreddies. Dam it, they were taken out of the same box and turned 45 degrees!  The 'better bit' of this example is that someone, somewhere got so upset that Diamond Shreddies had become more successful, they started a campaign to bring back 'Square Shreddies'. It was a success…it gave birth to the Diamond and Square Shreddies Multi-Pack. Brilliant. Just Brilliant. And bizarre at the same time.

It goes to show there are no new ideas. It's just how you present them to the public. Even the mighty Apple didn't have a new idea initially. There were hundreds of mp3 players on the market, yet we chose them. They just gave us a reason to buy one. 'An entire music collection in your pocket'. They kept the plate spinning as people moved to the phones, and kept them both spinning with newer, updated, faster and slicker models as we moved to the iPad and above. My question to you would be, how much harder are you going to have to work to spin your original plates as well as the shiny new ones you want to spin?

One of the key things that happened during the Third Doctors time, Pertwee's Doctor was portrayed as a 'dapper man of action' which was a stark contrast to his wily but less action-oriented predecessors. It was almost against type as Pertwee was very well known from comedic acting both on TV, film and radio. Here was a funny man playing things straight whilst the previous Doctor had been a serious actor playing for comedy.

It reflected a time where people wanted to be lost in an action packed environment and forget about the drab world around them. Times were getting tough and the 'free love' and laid-back life of the 1960's seemed a hell of a long time ago, as how the country was being run, how businesses were being run and how we interacted with our friends across the water, were changing and all beginning to bite at the same time. This Doctor was a 'premium product' packed into a budget box. Velvet jackets, capes, fedora's and frilly shirts were the Doctors signature. Here was an alien that dressed to be noticed. He was the 'Bond' of Doctors. By dressing the way he did, he gave an illusion of a debonair and sophisticated man with an excellent self grooming regime, whilst underneath harbouring a rough and tumble no-nonsense physicality.

I'd like to reflect on that a moment. In business we often see businesses that are hard as nails on the exterior but have a soft underbelly and crumble when put under pressure. The successful ones are the ones that are attractive, well drilled, react, cope and deliver surprises when the pressure is on. There is way too much relied upon when it comes to what something looks like. Don't get me wrong, it is pretty important, it's just that it's not the b-all and end-all. A straight Banana tastes the same as a curvy one. Misshapen carrots, turnips, potatoes and fruits, still taste of carrots, turnips, potatoes and fruit. Customers and clients do buy with their eyes and feelings, but if the business, the product or the service doesn't deliver on value or what is a reasonable expectation, then this leads to bitter disappointment and unwanted surprises. It becomes a Ferrari with a Robin Reliant engine. Looks good…massively disappointing to drive. Don't be that kind of business. Be the Aston

Martin that overdelivers, over performs and surprises the many, and not the few. (Cue car buffs getting upset at that last sentence.)

Talking of the 'many', it is well remembered that Pertwee took the franchise to the people. He was probably the first Doctor to be mobbed when in public. He was becoming 'rockstar' famous. Children loved him. Dad's were a little jealous and Mum's thought he was a little hot for an older man. Pertwee connected more with the viewing public than his two predecessors. Even after his tenure as the TV Timelord, he would openly talk about his time on the show and would spend a lot of time talking with fans from around the world. In my opinion this is where 'proper fandom' began. 'Dalekmania' was now long gone. So for an actor to have a connection with the public could only be good thing. It helped the show as other bigger, better and slicker shows began to appear.

It's here that we find another lesson, that perhaps gets lost in our technology driven world. Back in the late 60's and through to the early 70's we really didn't have technology. Not as it's known today. We sit and think that typing a few words on a social media platform is real connection. It's not. I'm really sorry to disappoint. Whilst it's great that I can connect with someone on the opposite side of the world within seconds and yes, I'm privileged and very lucky to be living in a time that allows me to do that, does that person actually know me? Do they like me? Do they really want to connect with me? Am I numbers game? Have I just entered a competition in dick-measuring when it comes to how big peoples followings are? Probably. And because of that I am just 'noise'.

When you look at businesses that have failed in the last 10 years, they have failed for many reasons but there is a clear lesson that keeps appearing and reappearing. Connection with it's customers. The collapse of toy giant Toys R Us was mainly discussed as it's failure to grapple with the online battle it faced. Whilst that is partly true, I know having talked to many mums and dads and even from my own experiences that the company lost touch with it's customers. And when I put it like that, you should be staggered. The biggest thing that kept popping up were the huge spaces they had to pay for in out-of-town buildings. It cost too much, it was unsustainable. Yet as I write this one of the most popular places that are situated in out-of-town areas are pubs and bars with fun houses for children. From there, some have begun trampoline parks, where kids have birthdays and just 'go-to' at the weekend or during holidays because mum and dad can have a little bit of 'quiet'. Here is the most ridiculous thing…why didn't Toys R Us actually do this? Become a destination for kids and families to go to? It would have been a captive audience. Isn't it a simple idea when I say that?

It's just a staggering lack of thought and imagination that led Toys R Us to crumble. As a child I loved going there with my Grandparents. We weren't rich, and often we would leave empty handed, but I could look at the latest toys and games. The latest figures and the latest bikes. So don't lose that connection with your customers and clients. You don't need an email list of millions or thousands. You don't need a Facebook following of hundreds or even hundreds of thousands. As author Austin Kleon, in his book 'Show Your Work' says, "You want hearts, not eyes." Have 20 people that will run through brick walls for you and tell the world how bloody amazing you are rather than 200 people who just view you as noise.

Talking of hearts and not eyes, this Doctor eventually gave us one of the most beloved companions that is sadly no longer with us. However in the journey to get there, the series was once again brave and perhaps a leader when it came to it's portrayal of women. His initial companion was UNIT scientist Liz Shaw (Caroline John). She first appears in the first serial of the this Doctor (1970), Spearhead from Space, having been drafted from the University of Cambridge as a scientific advisor to UNIT. She was portrayed as an accomplished scientist, an expert on meteorites with degrees in medicine and physics, and a dozen other subjects. Her extensive training, however, is still pale in comparison to the Doctor's own knowledge of the universe and scientific principles far beyond those of Earth. Sceptical at first of UNIT's ability to defend against alien invasion, Shaw changes her mind when she encounters the newly regenerated Doctor and becomes involved in defeating the plans of the Nestene Consciousness and its animated plastic Autons.

Liz continues to work with the Doctor and UNIT through other adventures where the Doctor also encountered Section Leader Elizabeth Shaw, an alternative version of the scientist in a parallel universe. She eventually resigns from UNIT and returns to Cambridge; there was no "farewell scene" on screen for Liz, with her departure simply being announced by the Brigadier at the beginning of Terror of the Autons. She reportedly told the Brigadier that all the Doctor really needed was someone to pass him his test tubes and tell him how brilliant he was. She probably wasn't wrong. But the reason I mention her and feel that it's correct that I write about her, is that since the first Doctor, Liz Shaw was the first woman companion to be given a strong personality and prove to people that women of that time weren't just dumb-assess that always asked "What does that mean Doctor?". We're talking the early 1970's where racism and sexism were rife yet here, admittedly for a short time was a TV show showing a strong woman and that she was the main characters equal. A shame we had to wait nearly 40 years for that to happen again. But it proved that at some level it was ahead of it's time in an era where those feelings that a woman could do the same job as a man were laughed out of the building. (Perhaps they knew something about a future Prime Minister towards the end of the decade?)

It shows that being forward thinking and giving people what they want too soon can be difficult. I guess we weren't ready for this in 1970 as Caroline John was quickly replaced as discussed and there are various stories as to why, but we were immediately served up some of the same as the previous two Doctors when wide-eyed Jo Grant, (Katy Manning), joined the Timelord who then continues to accompany the Doctor after he regains use of his ship, the TARDIS. Within the series narrative, Jo is a junior civilian operative for UNIT, is assigned as an assistant to the Doctor. Once he regains use of his time machine, she accompanies him in travels across time and space. Jo eventually departs the Doctor's company in the 1973 show The Green Death having fallen in love with a human professor. Manning and Pertwee enjoyed a close working relationship; Manning felt this added to the success of the partnership between Jo and the Third Doctor. Though her character was criticised for not being a progressive interpretation of a woman, Manning felt both that feminism was not a contemporary concern and Jo had her virtues aside from her intelligence, such as her loyalty. Her last episode personified some of the subject matters that the series was now tackling on a weekly basis. It tackled subjects such as corporate greed and chemical waste. Something we still haven't got a handle on, but in the environment of a children's weekly science fiction show, it may interest you that during the early to late 1970's the show attracted a 60% adult viewership. Perhaps the message wasn't going into a 7-year-olds ears, but it seems it didn't with their parents either. Shame. But it showed that there were levels and subjects that this show could handle with great grace and aplomb if it put its mind to it.

In a business sense, taking a backward step is fine. As mentioned, the character of Jo Grant seems like a backward step compared to Liz Shaw and in the cold light of day of 2019, yes, it is. But was the world really ready for a woman to be equal to their male counterpart? No. Sometimes being first isn't always good. Recognising a problem that needs solving before the bigger population are ready to realise that problem even exists can lead to wasted money, time and effort. It's a shame. Here was a perfect opportunity to promote feminism, on a public platform every Saturday tea-time. It just didn't 'work' for whatever reason. Wether it was the actor, the writers, the production team or those higher up, this was a situation that just didn't work out and going back to what had always worked is more than justifiable. In business it's ok to take a step back if it means you make that step forward at a later date. Not everything works and providing there is a learning, taking a step back to take a step forward is a good thing. Don't let anyone else tell you otherwise.

His final companion was intrepid journalist Sarah Jane Smith (Elisabeth Sladen). This was for many a defining moment in their childhood. Not as openly intelligent as Liz Shaw, or as stereotypical as Jo Grant, Sarah Jane Smith would prove to be, arguably, the most popular companion in the show's history. She would be the first companion to get her own show, (K9 and Friends. Dreadful. Just Dreadful.), but be given a second chance in the franchise some thirty years later and have an impact on a brand new generation of children. I'm not sure where the business lesson is in this one, but something compels me to write about something loosely based on what I said about the Second Doctor. You don't want to be the guy to follow the guy. You also don't want to go back when you were successful previously. Or do you?

The character of Sarah Jane Smith crossed over the time of Pertwee to Tom Baker. And it's also here that companions continued, in the main, to 'crossover' with different lead characters. Primarily to give people continuity but also act as a reassurance that not everything was changing even though the lead character had changed their face and personality. It's a reflection in business that when top management change, (unless you're a football manager), or that when businesses change hands and leadership that the core of the management team is kept on to see that there is continuity in day-to-day operations. It just makes it easier for everyone. But when someone leaves only to return some time later, that can be a gamble for both parties. The one that has really worked in living memory is of course, Steve Jobs. His return started a previously unseen stratospheric rise to dominance in business terms, and perhaps we won't see that again in my life time. On a smaller scale, it could be done. The right person, with the right heart, the right messages, the right skills and the ability to see the past for what it really is. Experience and nothing more.

People can not live on reputation alone and as previously said about the Second Doctor, there will be as many people willing you to succeed as there are willing for you to fail. Succeed, and the fact you've been away will soon all be forgotten. In Sarah Jane

Smith's case she reappeared in the instantly forgettable Five Doctors story but more memorably in the Tenth Doctor's story, School Reunion. Well written and well acted, it was like time had never passed. Because of the successful return and clamour for more of the fan favourite companion, head writer Russel T Davies gave her, her own show, 'The Sarah Jane Adventures' where she entertained a new generation of children on the BBC. It was a show that was full of important topics for children, mixed with aliens, space and time travel and effectively was a 'Dr Who-Lite' programme.

The character was probably the right character for the right time. Her mix of eccentric 70's clothing, her bravery, her intelligence and humour were the right balance at that time. It was the best of Liz Shaw and Jo Grant, rolled into one. A strong, but feminine companion. An equal and solid counsel for the Doctor and when it was needed by our window into the mind of the Doctor at others. It's good for businesses to have. Not everyone is built like Branson, Jobs, Gates and Musk. Not every leader wants the limelight and sometimes it's down to someone else in the organisation to take the lead and be the 'face' of the business. Not everyone is born to lead and that's OK. There are many who have made a career out of being someone's number 2, a second in command. In the same breath not every number 2 will do well when they have to step up. You just have to look at football management to see that. So when for whatever reason, someone as important as a Sarah Jane Smith leaves a business to spread their wings, you must let them do so with gratitude. And when they are ready to come back or you are ready to go back, just remember what I suggested earlier. The past is just that. The past. It counts for nothing other than experience.

One of the last few things for this Doctor, is that we need to talk about technology. Something that undoubtedly will rear it's head again before we finish all of the Classic Series of Doctors.

In Pertwee's case we need to talk about the technology that the Doctor uses and the technology of colour and special effects. All had a lasting effect on the series and all will have lasting effects on your business.

Firstly lets talk about the fact that this Doctor was a 'proper geek'. He loved making stuff. He made the 'Whomobile', which Pertwee himself actually owned after it had finished being used in production. A futuristic car that could fly! Wow! Why doesn't that stuff exist in 2019?

But it was a sign of the times as if you look at it in the cold light of the day, admittedly it didn't fly, but it was a part working prototype that Pertwee did in fact drive around the streets of London gaining astonished looks. He also had 'Bessie' which was a bright yellow soft top of a car that wouldn't have looked out of place with the first Model T Ford's. And it was quick. One of the first 'suped-up' cars of it's time. The show began to reflect the technology and the concerns it gave people. Stories reflecting robots and computers taking over the world weren't new, it's just that people had started to fear them. Some of the scariest shows in my opinion were the ones that followed the Autons, (a villain they would bring back for the 2005 re-boot), where shop dummies came to life and killed people. People could then be replicated and replaced. It worried people, rightly or wrongly. The technological effects that damaged environments, whether they were ours or an alien planet, their message was the same. In 2019 we have concerns regarding fracking and digging in places we really shouldn't be…all in the name of advancement.

Technology has had a big impact on how we do business now. We can connect with, go to, come from, talk to and ignore people faster than ever before. We are living in a time that if we're honest, we don't know where it will stop. The Doctor always tried to make sure that humanity had a say in how it's future is affected and by not allowing the technology to overtake the human race. Perhaps now is the time to look at your business and have a conversation with yourself and your team about wether technology has taken over your business, and maybe you are now missing that 'human touch'; the thing that we all need. People buy from people. Automation is great...to a point. Use technology as it's meant to be used, and not to the detriment of your business position.

Now why have I touched on colour? Colour always has been and will be revolutionary. It can make a business look old and tired, or give the same business the chance to look modern and vibrant. How? Well it's all down to the logo's and the colours that you use. The 70's were well known for using quite ridiculous colours together. The first house I bought had an avocado coloured bathroom suite with marine blue tiles. I bought it in 2000 and within 24hrs I had no functioning bathroom. No chance I was going to have a bath or a sit down in that! Colours and logo's make us feel something. Some of the most famous ones in the world actually have some genuine psychology behind them, and if it's good enough for them, it's good enough for you.

A big part of a strong corporate image is having a strong corporate colour. This means there is generally one dominant colour used in all aspects of your corporate image. This dominant colour is used consistently in everything you do and it forms the basis of the business' promotional material. Different colours evoke different emotions and it is important to choose an appropriate colour for your business. Darker colours tend to give a stronger, more established feel, hence a lot of law firms and accountants use dark blues, browns and even black as their corporate colour. Lighter colours tend to reflect a more modern look and feel and they are often favoured by businesses in the creative fields.

This is an area where you need to take the advice of a good graphic designer. Decide what image you want to portray and then get them to turn it into colour.

Colours, like most aspects of corporate branding, can go in and out of fashion so your corporate colours will need to be changed periodically. Just like a logo, they have a finite life span. Make sure the colour you choose can be used consistently in all printing and advertising as some colours are harder and more expensive to reproduce. Orange is one prime example of this; you can end up with a lot of variations which may erode the overall strong and consistent image you are trying to portray.

Here are some examples of 'colour psychology':

**Red:**
Emoting strength, passion and excitement

**Use in marketing terms :**
Used extensively in food terms to trigger appetite
Conveys a strong energy
Attracts attention and adds visibility

**Companies that use it:**
Virgin
Coca-Cola

**Yellow:**
Emoting intellect, joy and energy

**Use in marketing terms:**
Conveys positivity, high energy and optimism
Stimulates creativity and attracts customer attention
Indicates fun and a cheerful brand

**Companies that use it:**
McDonalds
Ferrari

**Blue:**
Emoting loyalty, trust and intelligence

**Use in marketing terms:**

Considered the most popular brand colour
Suggest high loyalty and precision
Closely associated to intelligence and trust

**Companies that use it:**
Ford
Dell

**Green:**
Emoting freshness, growth and safety

**Use in marketing terms:**
Is considered the easiest for human vision
Used to project an easy, relaxed image and
environment
Extensive use for environmental projects

**Companies:**
Starbucks
Body Shop

This stuff really works. Because not only did this
Doctor have a new title sequence, but they created a
new diamond shape logo at the same time. This was
to run for 10 years until 1980, at which point it was
ripe for a refresh and a new design. Just proving an
earlier point that as humans we are better at
accepting change quicker than you think.

And the last part of this section were the advancements in video technology. I'm going to be honest here. A lot of Pertwee's era doesn't fair so well given the advancement of time. More so than the black and white episodes before them. The quality of the film wasn't up to scratch and some of the green screen stuff was just laughable. It was a programme of it's time doing the best it could do with the budget it had. Where as nowadays, producers and directors are smarter with what can be done and can't be done on a budget, trying to achieve cinematic effects on a TV budget back then was never going to happen. And oddly as I see it now, I don't think we realise how good we have video technology. Affordable, cheap and quick...and on our phones.

The power of video is in our hands. Or pockets. Or bags. Or wherever we put our mobile phones. These devices mean we can take video footage whenever and however we like. There are actual cinematic releases being filmed on iPhones as we speak, such is the quality of the technology in these devices. So why aren't you using video to attract your best clients and customers? They don't have to be of Marvel Studio proportions, but everyone that owns a business should realise that they also need to be their own media company as well. Putting out what they want, when they want and no longer waiting for a film crew to rock up.

Now before videographers come and throw stuff at me, not for one minute am I suggesting that everyone do their own. No. Far from it. What I'm suggesting here is the behind the scenes stuff that let the customers into what really goes on. Every company should have a video filmed professionally to show their clients why they're different to everyone else. It shows personality and professionalism. What people don't want to see are videos with emoji's, rants and funny faces on. Does nothing for your business unless you are an emoji making, angry clown. Your first set of videos will be dodgy as hell, but the more you do, the slicker you get, the more relaxed you are, the better they become. Just don't use any model dinosaurs like Pertwee's era. (Check that out on YouTube, trust me you'll laugh.)

And finally we move onto the greatest of all nemesis for this Doctor. The Master. Originally played by Roger Delgado, The Master was the opposite to the Doctor. Where the Doctor wanted to live in peace, The Master wanted to tear things up, start a riot, rule a planet or two and destroy everything that was good with anything. A man of similar intellect, devices and gadgets, even having his own TARDIS that could change into something other than a blue Police Box, he would usually be behind a plot of some kind of evil only for the Doctor to interfere and halt his plan. It was a great addition to the show and from a personal point of view, one of the best villains that the show has ever had. But from a business point of view, it goes to only highlight what I've said in a previous chapter about competition. Except this time, this type of competition should allow you to 'raise your own game' and be better.

We all need competition in business. We just do. That's why I don't get, 'lock-out networking groups' entirely. If you're scared of competition then it's perfect for you, but not for the other people in the room. You see we are all human. And when we are not challenged or motivated, we tend to rest on our laurels. We can therefore sometimes slip below a standard we set ourselves. And before the self righteous amongst you say, "No, not I...": bollocks. Absolute rubbish. We do. We just don't openly admit it.

If we have competition we have to be on our 'A' game all the time otherwise we won't generate anything. Recently I sat in an event where there were three other coaches in the room. They all introduced themselves to the great and the good before I did, and by the time they'd finished I'd played 'Cliche Bingo'. They'd all come up with all the 'business coaching cliches' that I thought were possible. My mission? To introduce myself better than they had.

And I did. They had all tried giving their services the "big I am" and 'you should buy my stuff'. Me? I stood up and briefly spoke on the demise of another local company that had fallen by the wayside because they had lost touch with reality and hard work. If they didn't want to end up like that, then they should have a chat with me. I filled my three 1-2-1 appointments within seconds with some asking for a chat afterwards. The others? Handing their cards to each other. Competition is good. Always knowing and humbly understanding you are equal is good and will keep your feet on the ground. Allow others opinions of you and your business to be higher than your own. Whilst its flattering, don't buy into the hype. The minute you start telling yourself you are better than your competition, is the same moment you begin to lose connection to who you serve and what you're about. A business is not about you. But its starts with you. And in that order. The people that you serve are first.

After 4 years and 128 episodes, Pertwee decided to move on. After falling out of the TARDIS on his very first episode, he falls to the ground in his last TV moments as the Timelord. An emotional conversation between himself and his assistant Sarah-Jane ensues, breaking the hearts of children everywhere. And just as the 'regeneration' is about to take place, The Brigadier utters the words, "Well...here we go go again...", which was odd as he'd never seen a regeneration before!?

Let's take a quick look at the summary of the lessons with the Third Doctor:

1. **Doing what you can within a budget is a 'Golden Rule in Business'.** There are many businesses that have fallen over by trying to do something without any real control of their budget. In this case production costs had to be brought under control and many of the stories were situated on earth because it was cheaper. For it's day it still delivered a quality (of sorts) product. I always encourage clients to look at their costs and reduce by 10% every quarter, but WITHOUT doing damage to service, the product or the customer journey.

2. **Moving away from core principles and values is a risk.** The decade in which this show inhabited was a period of massive upheaval and change. And like its predecessors it needed to change to stay relevant, but this was the biggest change since the shows inception. Moving away from history and scientific discoveries was a risk. In this case it tried to make commentary on things that were becoming an issue such as corporate greed and green issues. You could argue it was a good call as the audience had grown up with the show

and those children were now teenagers or adults, so exploring those issues was very relevant to its audience.

3. **If you diversify, make sure you're spinning the right plates**. Following on from the last point, in business if you diversify or branch out into something different it's very important that you keep the original plate spinning. The diversification may not work, or work as well as hoped, so ensuring that the core part of the business doesn't topple can be tricky but absolutely necessary.

4. **There are no such things as new ideas**. The show had now been going 11 years and the formats of the stories had not really changed. It was still a story over 5 or 6 parts. But it really wasn't about Time and Space anymore. It was more of an Alien Invasion type of show. Yet the viewing figures were hitting tens of millions now. It's how you present something that is often the best way to make it look like a new idea. Take a look at the Shreddies video and it's associated videos : https://youtu.be/m5ds7WzVeew

5. **If you look flash, make sure the product or service backs it up**. Pertwee had been dressed as a dapper man of action. It would have been disappointing if he'd got beat every time he had some rough and tumble. So are you a business

that looks good but delivers a low quality product and service? If you are, sort yourself out. If you're a business that looks budget, but delivering a high quality product or service, you could be short changing yourself and the business. Tony Robins talks about human needs. Two of them being stability and surprises. We like things to be how they should be. If you buy something you perceive to be of quality and it's not, then you are disappointed. Which leads into the category of nasty surprises. But if you buy something you perceive to be of value and it exceeds the expectations, then you are pleasantly surprised and that goes a very long way. But as an aside, I want you to also remember this. A surprise quickly becomes standard. Therefore is no longer a surprise. Always aim to exceed expectations, as it's a key strategy when trying to grow a business.

6. **Connect on a personal level with your customers**. In a world with social media, we think we are having connection with our customers. We're not. We're just playing at it. Actual face-to-face time is on it's way back folks! You heard it here first. And don't just talk to people who want to pat you on the back and say how wonderful you are. Speak to the people that didn't buy. That didn't enjoy your service or product and listen. Just listen. Because in there, buried in all the

mess, are golden nuggets for your marketing and your business.

7. **Backwards steps are sometimes needed to move forwards**. At this particular point in time, neither the BBC or the viewing public were probably ready for a 'strong intelligent woman' to be part of the programme and for whatever reason they chose to take a step back to type. However when the stereotype moved on, they were replaced with not such a large leap of faith. There was balance. For the programme they introduced a companion that was very feminine but smart and strong at the same time. It was the combination of the last two, and became acceptable to the BBC and the viewing public at large as they became one of the most popular characters in the shows history. So sometimes, just sometimes moving forwards and then back, shouldn't be seen as a defeat, but more of a postponement until you find the right balance to move forward.

8. **If you were successful once, going back to something can be a risk**. I guess this is a legacy thing. People look at the past, successful times with rose-tinted glasses and we even do that ourselves as we like to self-edit. So you need to think, long and hard about going back to something that holds a successful period of your life. The past is the past, view it as experience

and as we all know, things, people and outside influences change. Have they changed too much for you to go back?

9. **Colours and Logo's**. I've already mentioned that humans are better at adapting to change than we give ourselves credit for. So take a look at the colours and logo's your business uses. Do they truly reflect the business you are in, or the times that we live in?

10. **Competition is inspiring**. If you use it as a way to improve yourself and your business, you're using it well. You're good. (You must be, you're listening to this). But to be better you must always be aware of what others doing and how you can supersede that. If you stand still, you're going backwards and failing. Don't be afraid of it... embrace it.

# The Fourth Doctor

Yes, we're still in the 1970's, and it's 1974 to be precise. The year I was born. The year a labourer became the Fourth Doctor. For full disclosure, my Doctor. The year Dr Who was about to be taken to several new levels. This was to be it's best of times, the beginning of it's worst of times and the longest of times. This was where one man, would become a new benchmark for everyone else to follow. This would be where fantasy and reality became very blurred. This was when Tom Baker became the Doctor.

I would have hated to have lived in the 70's. And by live in the 70's, I mean actually understand what the hell was going on, like my parents. It seemed such a turbulent time. You could say that as I write this, we are in turbulent times now with us leaving Europe as opposed to joining it. And as a country we were spending a lot of time navel gazing and fighting amongst ourselves, rather than just getting on with stuff. I guess in 40-odd years, not a lot has changed in those respects, but the Tom Baker 'era' was to hit heights that the show would never see again, at least not for a very long time. Baker portrays the fourth such incarnation as a whimsical and sometimes brooding individual whose enormous personal warmth is at times tempered by his capacity for righteous anger.

His 172 episodes covering nearly a seven year span and finally hung his scarf up in what would be seen as a period where an end was in sight. It certainly wasn't down to him that it entered a phase from which it would take decades to recover, but it could be argued that he outstayed his welcome, that one year too long. In the same way that Arsene Wenger managed Arsenal Football Club, he came in with a breath of fresh air, became a legend very quickly, but towards the end found that perhaps, just perhaps, things had moved on a bit too quickly for him and that his 'legend' had been tainted ever so slightly.

However some 30-odd years on, Baker still has a huge presence in fandom circles and is often seen receiving (and thoroughly enjoying), the adulation of Dr Who fans the world over. Did it ruin a varied career? Probably. Was it coloured by rose-tinted glasses? Certainly. Is he considered a legend? Very definitely.

And so I guess we should open this part, with us looking forwards to the present day and not backwards through his time as a Timelord.
1)  Because it makes it fun for me, and
2)  Dr Who is the subject of time travel for crying out loud, so lets use it.

In 2013, amongst rumour, counter rumour and more rumour the actor was escorted into a studio somewhere in Cardiff, under intense secrecy. Tom Baker was to appear in the 50th Anniversary show, "The Day of the Doctor". I was fortunate enough to be sat in a VUE cinema in Worcester with my son, (aged 10 at the time), when his distinctive voice bellowed out of the digital surround speaker system in a sold out, live screening of the episode. I, along with a huge proportion of the audience, 'whooped' with joy as 'our Doctor' appeared on the screen properly since he left in 1981. Now when I say, 'our Doctor', I'm talking people of a certain age. I was just hitting 40, and Tom Baker became the Doctor, eleven days after I was born, but when I did get into Dr Who, he very quickly became 'my Doctor'. I was nearly 7 when he regenerated and this was the very first time I had seen this. But I always have an absolute fondness for a man, who not only became a complete 'Rockstar' when it came to the character, but for some reason, transcended the show and the world in which it inhabited.

I also mentioned, 'appeared on the screen properly since he left in 1981'. This was true, as his previous appearance in 'The Five Doctors', a 20th anniversary special, was as a wax-work dummy in the promotional pictures and bits of video footage used from an unaired episode called 'Shada'. After initially agreeing to take part, Baker declined to return so soon after his departure from the series two years before, saying in 2014, *"I didn't want to play 20 per cent of the part. I didn't fancy being a feed for other Doctors—in fact, it filled me with horror."* That quote alone should should tell you more than you need to know about what Tom Baker thought of himself when it came to be the lead of this show.

So having started at the end, lets "Vwoop, Vwoop", (that's the noise of the TARDIS by the way), to the 8th June 1974, where I am literally 11 days old, and Tom Baker appears on the floor of a room at UNIT Headquarters to replace Jon Pertwee. The third Doctors tenure finished strongly with an average of 8 million people watching, but this new incarnation is generally regarded as the most recognisable of the

Doctors and one of the most popular, especially in the United States.

The Fourth Doctor's eccentric style of dress and speech – particularly his trademark long scarf and fondness for Jelly Babies sweets – made him an immediately recognisable figure and he quickly captivated the viewing public's imagination. Producer Phillip Hinchcliffe has often stated that the Fourth Doctor's 'Bohemian' appearance and anti-establishment views appealed to older, college-age students. However just like the second Doctor, people voiced their 'fear of change' with letters to the papers and the Radio Times, with quotes of "...he's too stupid for words...", "My little boy didn't like the new Doctor. He thought he was too silly..." a personal favourite of mine which was, "I would like him calmed down down a bit, because he's crazy." This was balanced out a bit with some praise, but as I mentioned in another chapter, we have to be honest with ourselves when it comes to criticism. Become the thermostat rather than a thermometer.

Tom Baker, the actor, had an an unusual path to the role. At the age of 15, the Liverpudlian studied to become a monk but lost his faith by the age of 21. How did that happen? According to his autobiography he wanted to break each of the Ten Commandments in order, something that would have certainly been frowned upon. He went on to do his National Service in the Royal Army Medical Corps for two years, where he got the taste for acting by entertaining troops. He went on to study acting at the Rose Buford College of Speech and Drama and it was the late 60's when he became an actor full time. Having worked at the National Theatre, then headed by Sir Laurence Olivier, he went on to do TV work, appearing in Dixon of Dock Green and Z-Cars. His first film break was the role Gregoria Rasputin in the film Nicholas and Alexandra after Olivier had recommended him for the part. For me I saw his role Koufax, the villainous sorcerer, in Harryhausen's 'The Golden Voyage of Sinbad' as something else. He was sharing the screen with plasticine monsters and real life actors. Almost a great grounding for Dr Who.

However he found himself out of work and sent a letter to his old friend and director Bill Slater, asking if he knew of anything going. Slater at the time was BBC's Head of Serials, and recommended Baker to then Producer Barry Letts. At the time Baker was working on a building site and after meeting with the suits at the BBC and getting the job, he went back to work for the rest of the day to finish off. It was the start of something very rock and roll.

Baker made the part his own and viewing figures would quickly hit and surpass the numbers at the time of Dalekmania. The Fourth Doctor's time enjoyed a significant boost in viewing figures, averaging between 8 and 10 million viewers in just his first year (20–25 percent of the entire viewing audience of

Britain). By 1979, the figures averaged between 9 and 11 million, going as high as 16.1 million for the final episode of a story called 'City of Death' (though this was during the technicians strike from ITV which meant the BBC was the sole broadcaster on the air for several weeks).

Look at me, nearly 1400 words into this chapter, and no business lessons. Well actually there is. Baker was a good actor. You are not considered 'shabby' if Sir Laurence Olivier recommends you for roles, but he hit a 'rough patch'. In fact when Baker met with BBC bosses, he had no knowledge of the role for which he'd been asked to discuss. He arrived with a copy of 'Wind in the Willows' in his pocket and spent most of the meeting time, discussing the morality of good versus evil for children. It's exceptional when you think about it, as the producers had originally wanted an older male to play the role, but agents and actors turned the BBC down because of lack of availability or lack of interest. You might think I'd talk about how you 'pitch' for a gig, but the lesson I want to talk about is how Baker got out of his rough patch by reaching out and asking for help. It's something that we should take note of in business and something I'm quite passionate about. As business owners or self-employed people, we are very proud people. We have 'chosen' to take a path that many don't want to. It is, when you're in it, arguably harder working for yourself than working for someone else. We wake up thinking about our business and go to sleep with relative amounts of success or failure thinking about our business. And because we're proud, we look at asking for help as a sign of weakness. It's not. It's a brave thing to do and for those that have done, perhaps the difference between staying in business or going out of business. Let me clarify what I mean by 'asking for help'. There are two things here.

Firstly there's the 'I'm in trouble, what can you do to help me?' Type of asking. Then there's the 'Could you recommend me to someone please?' Type of help. Neither should be looked at in a negative way. Let's deal with recommendations first. Getting recommendations and allowing people to recommend you is one of the cheapest forms of marketing on the planet. The hard work is already done. When someone comes to you via a good recommendation, they come to you having 'bought into' what you do, and how you do it. If it's an amazing recommendation, then there's a good chance they're bought into the price too, so any price objections are usually very low. Prompting people to recommend you can be a touch embarrassing, but you shouldn't view it as a weakness. There is a very good chance that the person recommending you, is probably your 'ideal customer or client' and will know more of 'your ideal customers and clients'. I'd say that's a great way to get an excellent return on investment. You do the job well for one person and they bring you four more.

(Just remember it can work the other way. Do it badly, and they'll tell ten people.)

Secondly, there's the 'I'm in a little bit of trouble, can you help?'. This is probably the braver of the two questions. There are lots of people out there that will help fellow business owners. (And remember there as many who won't…so just remember them!) At some point or other, they have been in the same place as you. They have made mistakes, rubbish cash-flow, not enough customers or clients coming through the doors, poor profits and big losses. Whatever the situation, it has never, not happened before. For all the competition out there, humanity in general still has many rays of light willing to reach out and help. You just have to ask.

I met a guy once that had all the tools and knowledge to help businesses promote themselves on the internet. A few weeks later, I woke to a message asking me for help. He had not slept for a few days and had only £30 in his bank account. I messaged back and we arranged a call for later that day. He was in a mess, both personally and financially. Situations had spiralled out of control and he messaged me because he didn't know who to turn to. We spent an hour and a half on the call. Two weeks later he had attracted enough work to get a regular income of £3000 per month. He now runs his own online PR business and has personally built my website from scratch. I received no money for the help I gave, but I wanted to because here was a man who was at rock bottom with nowhere to go. I've been there. It's horrible and lonely. But things began to turn around for me when I reached out and asked for help. So this was me 'paying it forward'. I don't tell you this for a 'pat on the back', I tell it you to show you that if you find yourself in a situation where you need help, then don't be afraid to ask. Look to people that you admire, that you've worked with or who know you. The worst thing you can do is to go back into your shell and say nothing. It's a spiral very few get out of. Baker wrote a letter…(you could write an email, send a text, send a PM or even use the phone in your hand for what it was originally designed for…speaking to people), asking someone wether there were any roles he could be considered for. He got the gig.

The first of Baker's stories, 'Robot', was not a classic. Truth be told, it had been written for Pertwee because all the elements were there. However this incarnation certainly took on its own 'style' and narrative. In fact many of the stories from his era are considered to be classics of the series, including The Ark in Space, Genesis of the Daleks, The Brain of Morbius, The Deadly Assassins and The Robots of Death. It took on some very 'gothic' tones with a sprinkle of 'Hammer House of Horror'. This was not a bad thing. Science fiction was changing and the budgets of the BBC were certainly not in the same ball-park as a certain movie that was due to smash all box office records and change the landscape of sci-fi forever in

1977. But until then Baker had a run of 3 years before the aftershocks were felt.

Regularly sighted as 'THE' Dr WHO, Baker took the whole 'rockstar thing' that Jon Pertwee had started and did it...well...better. You see Baker was the Doctor. The Doctor was Tom Baker. There was almost no dividing line. What you saw on screen is what you got in public. But notice I didn't say 'private', and we'll touch on that shortly. When asked if he minded for being known as 'The Doctor' as opposed to a good actor that appeared in movies like 'Educating Rita', he simply said, "No. I never rated my acting. My Doctor Who was just Tom. As soon as I started to say the lines, the children loved it. I said, "Hey! Who wants to act, when I can just be Tom?" A business lesson here is that every business owner or self employed person needs to learn, nay, absolutely remember, is that you are your business. Your business is the business of you. With social media and marketing as it is; websites, LinkedIn, Google, other search engines, Twitter, Facebook, etc...never has there been a time in society where you are not, 'on the clock'. Through technology you and your business are available to your customers and clients 24/7, 365 days of the year.

Amongst what must have been a gruelling filming schedule for the show, Baker was asked to appear at exhibitions, conferences, schools, switching Christmas lights on, opening fayres and virtually the opening of an envelope, as this was how you 'did' marketing in the 1970's. You couldn't upload a video, do a 'live' or post a picture of yourself in a toilet mirror pouting like an idiot. If you were a public figure, you had to be just that...public. And to his immense credit he made the character and the show accessible to everyone, widening it's appeal and broadening the audience. You just have to look at the numbers to see that it worked. It was a way of 'forgetting' all the stuff that was actually going on in the real world, which at times during the 1970's in the UK was quite depressing. The lesson here is genuine and whole hearted connection to your customers and clients.

That's one of two business lessons that I can see here and the one I want to discuss here is the danger of believing your own hype.

Baker for all intense purposes was obsessed by the role and from what you see and read about the actor, it was hardly a surprising trait of his personality. However he really thought he 'was the show'. For some that's an attractive trait and for others an absolute turn-off. Both confidence and humility have their merits, but both have their negatives. And both will attract a different type of person to your circle. In the business world, some maybe attracted to the loud-mouth, hurricane, confident and brash business person, (you're welcome...I've just described myself), as it can be seen as a sign of success. On the other hand others maybe attracted to someone who's quieter, more considered, more introvert but just as good as the loud mouth. It certainly can be argued that Baker at times thought he was bigger than the show.

Behind the scenes, and pulling on various different sources, Tom Baker, actor and private individual got increasingly difficult to work with. In many interviews, he felt he 'knew' the character better than anyone. Including the producers, directors and writers. He rubbed co-stars up the wrong way, married one of them, argued with directors and regularly changed scripts. He loved Barry Letts, and the violent tone of the stories produced by Letts' successor, Philip Hinchcliffe. Like Verity Lambert before him, Hinchcliffe in his first producers role, saw the series come under very heavy criticism at home from 'morality campaigners'. Concerns over violence during this early period led to a lightening of the tone and an erratic decline in both the popularity and quality of the series. Baker has described Hinchcliffe as "amazing" and identified that as his favourite period of his time on the series. He described Hinchcliffe's successor, Graham Williams, as "absolutely devoted" but lacking Hinchcliffe's flair and he acknowledged that his final producer on the series, John Nathan-Turner, made changes he didn't agree with and they "did not see eye-to-eye really about very much". Baker had become very controlling about the role and like Hartnell before him, thought he knew everything. He should and could have left at the end of William's tenure, but because it had become such a huge part of him and his life, he couldn't bring himself to fall on his sword just yet. And as future chapters may point to, he may have had a point about John Nathan-Turner, but we'll discuss that later.

In business no-one is bigger than the business itself. If you've built an empire, no matter how big or small, the behaviour that the business and it's employees exude and display can make or break a business in equal measure. Let's take a look at one of the most costly, (some deem it the 'Billion Dollar Blowout'), of speeches made by someone that thought he was bigger than his own business, a certain Gerald Ratner.

Ratner was the CEO of the Ratners Group, jewellers that shook up the usually stiff and inflexible jewellery market by aiming some of its products at the working class through a chain of shops known as "Ratners." Although the chain was widely ridiculed and considered "gaudy," "tacky" and "cheap" by the press and other jewellers, many wanting to buy jewellery and not break the bank flocked to the stores, turning Ratners into a household name throughout England in the 1980s.

This unprecedented move was primarily spearheaded by Gerald Ratner himself and it turned what was once a small, family-owned chain into a billion dollar business, threatening other jewellers the world over.

How? Well if everyone owns and wears jewellery, and it is sold cheaply to the mass-market, it loses much of its prestige and perceived value which has long made certain mostly worthless jewellery items extremely expensive. It was turning the industry on it's head.

Ratner started working for the company in 1965 when he was a fresh-faced teen. In the 19 years he worked for the company, it made almost no market headway. When he inherited the company in 1984, he expanded it from about 150 shops to over 2,000 in just six years, capturing over 50% of the UK's jewellery market. Ratner appeared to be a business prodigy. In his autobiography, **Gerald Ratner: The Rise and Fall… and Rise Again**, Ratner claimed that his success in the 1980s was down to an experience he had when he was younger at Petticoat Lane Market. At this market, Ratner noticed that it wasn't the vendors selling the best goods that got the most sales or interest from customers, it was the vendors who yelled the loudest and had the most garish, eye-catching displays.

Ratner eagerly applied this concept to his own business when he took over the Ratner Group in 1984, and he made sure that all of the shops in the Ratners chain had bright orange displays that loudly advertised their prices and deals. This, combined with the rock-bottom prices the chain was offering, saw sales explode.

It was at the peak of his company's success, Ratner was invited to speak to the Institute of Directors, a group of high-powered businessmen and journalists, about how he'd made his company so big so fast. This speaking engagement, which Ratner himself now refers to as "the speech," has since gone down as one of the biggest blunders in business history.

Though the speech was going well for a while, the fateful moment came when a person in attendance innocently asked Ratner how his company was able to afford to sell things so cheaply; his now infamous response was as follows:

"…We also do cut-glass sherry decanters complete with six glasses on a silver-plated tray that your butler can serve you drinks on, all for £4.95. People say, 'How can you sell this for such a low price?' I say, because it's total crap…", and followed it up by saying this about some earrings he sold with, "(they're) cheaper than an M&S prawn sandwich but probably wouldn't last as long."

Now whilst this doesn't sound as earth shattering as some views that have been held by people on Twitter in the last ten years, this was the 1980's. This was a huge business nationally and an entrepreneur that people believed in. When the story broke in the tabloids and on TV and Radio, the general public felt they had been taken for a fool. The effect on the company's profit were practically instantaneous.

Almost overnight shares in the company dropped by £500 million or around $800 million (about £936 million / $1.6 billion today) and customers began avoiding Ratners stores like the plague. The phrase "doing a Ratner" entered the English lexicon as a term for really screwing up.

Just a year after his speech, Ratners stores began closing down by the hundreds, resulting in thousands of jobs being axed. The company claimed that the dramatic loss of profits was due to "a shift in consumer spending habits," which is kind of true in a sense, but it's pretty obvious from the five hundred million pound punch to the gut they received just a year prior, that it was really due to 'that' speech.

(A quick note here - "a shift in consumer spending" - as I write this the High Street is 'struggling' and this same excuse is used as an excuse for a business falling over or collapsing. Perhaps it's also a remark that should be used for a level of incompetence or admitting they've made mistakes.)

Ratner resigned in November of 1992 and the company, in an effort to distance itself further from it's owner, unceremoniously re-branded themselves as the "Signet Group" in 2002.

Though his speech had cost his company hundreds of millions of dollars, Ratner himself came out of the scandal relatively unscathed, as noted in an interview with him, "I sold my shares on the day I left. I didn't make anything. The only good news was that the £1billion owed to the bank stayed with the company rather than me."

He then managed to acquire a few million pounds by mortgaging his house and investing the money in various business ventures, such as a health club business that he sold in 2001 for £3.9 million (adjusted for inflation about £5.6 million today or about $9.4 million). These days, he runs a jewellery business with an estimated value of about £35 million or $59 million. When he's not doing that, Ratner occasionally earns extra money by giving speeches at business conventions or mastermind groups.

So whilst Baker never, ever mocked the fans, and made sure that he was always seen to be doing the right thing, there are times when personal feelings and relationships need to be parked and do 'what's best for business' and the baton handed on. It must have been hard for Baker to 'give up' on something that had literally changed his life. He was the man to be recognised up and down the country, but that country and the people in it had changed without him noticing.

I've just mentioned 'handing over the baton', and so it's worth taking a quick look at this in terms of the show and business. As in many business style relationships there was a 'handover' period where

Barry Letts, producer for Jon Pertwee, handed over the show to Philip Hinchcliffe. Because the stories had already been commissioned and scripts written Bakers first series was really a retread of things that had been done before but were edited and altered to ease the viewers into a different style. The second of Baker's series were very definitely what they had always wanted. The first departure from the previous incarnation was a relatively short-lived one. It was in the form of the TARDIS crew, and the newly joined Royal Navy surgeon, Harry Sullivan. Because it was thought that an older man was going to play the Doctor, they had drafted the character in to be the 'heroic one' of the team. A little bit like in the 60's with some of the male companions of the first two Doctors. So although it made some interesting viewing, with two men being slightly 'alpha-male', Harry left at the end of Baker's first season. The only person that remained was Sarah-Jane Smith from the Pertwee era, and she was for all intense purposes, the fan favourite.

There should always be a time to 'handover' things. Wether you own and have sold a business or whether you are taking over in management somewhere, a short period of 'handover' time is a good thing. It's reassurance for those within the business and those that use the business. As I seem to keep banging on about, we can actually deal with change better than we give ourselves credit for but as Tony Robbins says, two of our human needs that we 'enjoy' are certainty and uncertainty. Change brings uncertainty and a handover period settles people and businesses down with some certainty.

When Sarah-Jane Smith chose to leave, (the actor and the character), she was quickly replaced by "Savage Tribeswoman', (squeezed into a very objectifying set of leathers), Leela, played by Louise Jameson. Now at first this sounds all quite sexist, but there were two genuine aspects to the character that perhaps don't garner much discussion for whatever reason. In this character was a strong woman, who could handle some rough and tumble just like the Doctor and any male companion before her. There was also the aspect of the 'Eliza Doolittle' to the Doctor's 'Professor Higgins' relationship. The drama could be said to be teaching young people some great aspects of society. In 2019 we're still struggling to come to terms with strong women and for people of any background to be able to better themselves. A shame this story was being told in the 1970's as we should look inwardly and wonder why we're still talking about this stuff right now.

Eventually she was replaced by the first "Timelady', Romana. Originally played by Mary Tamm, and then with the aid of an off screen regeneration by Lalla Ward, the character was considered a match for the Doctor's intellect. In fact it is suggested in their first meeting, she is actually superior to him, by passing her University exams first time, as opposed to 'scraping through with 52% second time around'. The character was sparingly used as his equal, but the intent was there by the writers, if not poorly delivered.

Women in business is probably another book on it's own, but the writers of Dr Who have always tried to 'push the boundaries' when comes to showing powerful or strong women. Admittedly it's not in the same bracket as some dramas that are currently being shown, but for it's place in time as a popular drama that was being seen by millions week in and week out, the issue of a strong woman was never a problem for the show. It was a second attempt to bring in a strong female equal and eventually we get one - just look at Doctor number 13...

The viewing figures were absolutely sky high, but things were changing and the BBC teams reacted to what was happening in a way that ended up potentially marking the beginning of the end for this Doctor and maybe the franchise.

In 1977, we were given 'Star Wars'. You may have heard of it? It changed the sci-fi landscape forever and would ultimately change the 'business' of sci-fi. How it was done. How quickly it could be done. The quality of what was done. The money that was spent on it. The money that could be made from it.

Polished and shiny imports started making their way to our screens on 'the other channel' in the form of

Battlestar Galactica, Buck Rogers and other such things. The Americans gave us C3-P0, R2D2, Twiki and Muffit. Dr Who gave us K9. A prop that repeatedly broke down and often had to be written out of stories because it just wouldn't work properly and cost the princely sum of £750 in the 1970's. That's £4525 in todays money! A huge sum for a remote control metal dog that doesn't connect to wifi or Bluetooth! And that doesn't include the bloke sat behind the set reading his lines! The show was beginning to follow other peoples rules. Something it had not genuinely done before. Sure there were influences and strong hints, but the show was now trying to compete on a playing field that was no longer level.

The next lesson for business here is the ability...nay choice, not to compete. Let's take a look at something we all know about. Clothes. For many years, the British public have wanted high brow, designer gear, often going for the cheap knock-offs that could buy and sell quite freely. We then had this next band of happy companies giving us what they thought were cheap prices for gear of reasonable quality and design. This was to be known as 'the middle ground'. Then we were introduced to Primark. One of the most successful clothing lines in the world. Derided by some as 'disposable fashion', it's bought fashion to the high-street for everyone. People are no longer mocked for buying Primark or 'Primarni' as its fondly called, but just accepted. Now why do I tell you this?

Well if you look at the 'middle ground' that wandered around with it's head up their own arse for many years, it's those retailers that are currently feeling the squeeze and are in various degrees of failure. Their message isn't strong enough. They don't know who they're marketing to and what their customers actual wanted. They've lost market share and are spending a ridiculous amount of time trying to be all things to all people. Trying to compete with those above them and those below them. By extension, the current state of Department Stores such as Debenhams and House of Fraser are in exactly the same place. They're not high end, and they're not bottom end. But all are trying to market to everyone. Market to everyone and you market to no-one. The thing to remember in business is that if there is a market for your product or service, you market to those people. And if you market to those people, it's absolutely necessary to remember what you are and who you are. If you are a budget brand you don't set up a shop in Harrods. And if you're you are a genuine Armani you don't set up on a market stall.

It's the ones that 'sit in the middle' that tend to struggle when top end and bottom end businesses get it right. Taking a look at the food retail industry, would it surprise you that in the 5 years after the financial crisis of 2008 that Aldi and Lidl grew their business very quickly? Probably not as people were looking for cheap alternatives. But would it surprise you that Waitrose and Marks and Spencers, both considered the high street version of 'top end' groceries, also grew? Tesco, Sainsbury, ASDA and Morrisons all lost market share and started a price war with...each other. Ridiculous really. But Aldi, Lidl, Marks and and Spencer and Waitrose all had strong messages about what they were, who they were for and what they could do for you. Their messages were about value of different kind. For the lower end it was a low price with surprising quality, whilst it was a higher price but guaranteed quality at the top end. Neither lost focus and if anything it refocused their marketing and brand values.

A little bit of an aside here, is the marketing that Aldi's did to help their growth. And I can loosely relate this to marketing Dr Who versus Star Wars or Buck Rogers as an example. On billboards, posters, TV spots and leaflets, Aldi spent most of their time comparing Apples and Oranges. Not literally you understand but metaphorically. What they did was so easy it was unreal, and for the life of me, still can't work out why the others didn't follow suit. As I write this, they're still doing it and it's just...simple. All they did was a basket or a trolley comparison. There would be a basket from one of the big brand supermarkets, with branded washing-up liquid, washing powder, crisps, butter, etc...all everyday items. And then they would have a basket or trolley of their own stuff. You see the problem is, depending on which side of the fence you're on, Aldi don't stock big branded products, they mainly stock their own sourced products. You see? Apples versus Oranges. It showed the value of the company as a business that offered low pricing with surprising quality and value. If somehow the marketing department at Doctor Who had been used to help promote the series as a value driven but surprisingly brilliant story telling show and 'manage' viewers expectations better then it wouldn't have been picking up the 'wobbly set' tag as big as it did. In turn perhaps producers wouldn't have tried so hard and spent money on effects when story telling and writers would have been a better allocation of the shows money.

Dr Who wanted to compete with the Americans and big screen sci-fi. It began to look cheap. As the producers began to try to keep pace with the technological developments on a shoestring budget, the quality of the stories and the effects began to wear thin. They haven't aged well. It began to 'do' what it wasn't good at. It began to forget to tell great stories. The ecological parables of the Pertwee era had given way to darker story lines but were as important if not more thought provoking. The story considered the 'best Tom Baker story' and the one repeated more than any 'Classic Who' stories is 'Genesis of the Daleks'. In this story the Daleks felt like they were back. Truth is they had never left, but after their creator Terry Nation had been unsuccessful in launching a 'spin-off' Dalek series, (what?!), and when writing episodes for the series up until this point, he almost 'phoned them in'. They followed the same plot lines, constantly rehashed. Genisis was different. With the back drop of genocide in other parts of the world and the memories of World War 2 still alive and kicking, this story looked at the Daleks creation on a planet with races fighting amongst each other and a psychopathic dictator looking for supremacy and domination. A little too close to home, but within the writing there is a moment that has been repeated more times than any, when Baker's Doctor is given the opportunity to destroy the Daleks by just touching two small wires. The moralistic stance is Baker at his best. Dr Who at it's best. So it was still educating and entertaining children and adults alike with or without dodgy effects.

And now to the end. Sometimes, just sometimes you outstay your welcome. Sometimes, just sometimes you won't listen. Sometimes you know what's best for business and that's the way it is.

We've seen it all before with someone, somewhere at some business or another. Painful isn't it?

So was Tom Baker's last year as the Doctor. Already not wanting to fall on his sword, the management of the show ended up taking 'his show' away from him. His team changed to three people. Two of the most annoying companions ever and Nissa, (which is also the name of a convenience store here in the UK).

They changed his costume to be brighter and less 1970's. And if you watch the last dozen episodes of the series with the knowledge that he was going, you can visibly see the anguish, tiredness and lack of energy in his performances. In his head this was his show. He was the franchise. But new producer John Nathan-Turner seemed to have other ideas and as the leader of the production, he tried too hard to match and do more than the other shows with what he had. He tried to give it the polishing a turd treatment even when his budget was £4.50 compared to an American budget of tens of thousands of dollars. We'll touch on this more in the next few chapters, but this was not a pretty end for a man who had lived, breathed and exuded Dr Who for 7 years.

He decided his time was up and as he fell to his TV death from a radio telescope on the 21st March 1981, he looked to his three companions and uttered the words "It's the end...but the moment has been prepared for..." As he motions towards a white clad figure, they merge and after TV trickery morph's into the figure of a young man that was more used to sticking his hand in a cows arse, than being a Timelord. Dr Who was about to get a bit weird...

Lets recap on the lessons from Bakers era:

1. **Ask for help**. It doesn't matter how new you are to business or how long in the tooth you are, asking for help and recommendations is NOT a

sign of weakness. I'd like you to consider that it's real life. People will help if you ask. Your happy customers, clients, suppliers all have a vested interest in you doing well, so don't be afraid to reach out as it may open new doors and new opportunities you'd not considered before.

2. **If you're going to be anything in business, it's be authentic**. But with that has to come an understanding. At no point ever in life, has anyone been liked by everyone. So this is why being authentic is a good thing, because some people will like what you do, how you do it and why you do it. Others won't. And that is fine.

3. **If you represent a business or a brand, you should always put them first**, even if you're stood in front of the business. Baker represented a show that millions of children watched week in and week out. He made sure he wasn't 'caught' smoking or with a beer in his hand. You control your media output and your own behaviour. Remember that.

4. **You are not bigger than any business or any brand**. Even if it is your own and it truly is your blood, sweat and tears that got you to where you are. Yes you may have views on how things should be done, but the words "We've always done it that way" are 6 of the biggest killer words to any business. When it's time to go...it's time to go.

5. **Strong women rock**. Fact.

6.  **Handing over the baton is always a good idea** and allows people time to accept change and the future.
7.  **Stop competing with apples if you're an orange**. Stop competing with oranges if you're an apple. Learn to make sure your message is consistent and that the customers you want are still wanting what you think they want.

# The Fifth Doctor

1981. The year I first became aware of the Toys R Us Christmas Toy Catalogue. The year I started following Wolverhampton Wanderers. The year I started watching cricket. The year a cricket loving, flannel wearing, ever so slightly too fast talking and high pitched blonde haired chap took control of the TARDIS.

This was Peters Davison's era. This was to be the beginning of the end. This is where it all started going horribly wrong.

After Tom Baker, the Fourth Doctor and the BBC had announced that he was leaving the role, the show's producers decided that the next Doctor was to be played by someone who presented something of a physical contrast to Baker and by an actor who was already firmly established in the British public's mind. The actor was to be Peter Davison and was chosen due to his 'critically acclaimed role' as Tristan Farnon in the BBC series All Creatures Great and Small, which had current Doctor Who producer John Nathan-Turner as it's line producer. It was not a choice that 'wowed' the BBC nor fans alike, but there was a reason behind it and we'll come to that later.

The Fifth Doctor's era was notable for a "back to the basics" attitude, in which "silly" humour (and, to an extent, horror) was kept to a minimum, and more scientific accuracy was encouraged by the producer. It was, at times, a darker and grittier series than the previous one, in part for an episode showing the death of one of his companions, Adric. It was also notable for the reintroduction of many of the Time Lord's enemies, such as the Master, Cybermen, Omega (a founding-father of the Doctor's home planet Gallifrey), the Black and White Guardians, and the Silurians. It was also more notable for the genuine tag of 'wobbly sets' and dodgier special effects than any series before it.

The fact that it did try it's best to go back to basics, unfortunately didn't help it. It made it worse. As a business lesson there is something to be learned from avoiding going back to basics. It isn't always the saving grace it could be. The idea behind the series was to entertain, educate and fill 25 minutes on a Saturday tea-time. Looking back at it now, they went back to trying to tell stories on a virtual 1960's budget but in the 1980's with stiff competition from the the glitzy and more glamorous million dollar American TV imports. They were always going to be second best as they simply weren't competing on the same level of a budget of any other sci-fi series in production. It could be said that over the next 8 years, by trying to take itself so seriously it made itself look like an utter joke.

When you go back to basics, there has be a realisation that the world moves on and things change. Whilst there will always be problems for businesses to solve, the way in which they solve them will change. It's like grated cheese. After many years of making our fingers and knuckles bleed on cheese graters, the manufacturer's of cheese graters now realise we can buy pre-grated cheese in bags. Therefore the market for cheese graters is not as big in certain places as they used to be. Does that make sense?

Take this book for example. I'm sat here writing this and imagining a lovely paperback with a lovely cover with a lovely smell. But I also have to realise that some people like to consume their books via Apps like Kindle. So book publishers going back to basics, can't go back to what they did even 5 years ago, because consumers choices have changed. (Also never assume that because a book is published, the writer is a multi-millionaire. JK Rowling is an exception.)

There is to a degree, a counter argument with what I've just written, which is that things do go around in cycles. An I agree with that to a point. Let's look at vinyl, it's made a comeback, but has it made the comeback that means it hits the levels of it's heyday? No. Downloads and other means of consuming music still outstrip the feel and sound of a vinyl record and so I could then argue it falls into one of two categories. Niche or novelty. Time will tell.

So Dr Who going back to basics, was a franchise trying to go back to the same basics of 1963 and trying to recapture a former glory. Nearly 18 years had passed and we all know how quickly the UK had changed in that time. TV had changed and the expectations had changed. Remember the onslaught of American imports? They were getting bigger and better and they had started moving away from sci-fi. 1980 gave us Buck Rogers in the 25th Century. Battlestar Galactica had finished but the US gave us Galactica '80 with Dick Van-Dyke's son being terrible. 1982 gave us Knightrider, a talking, stunt driving black Trans-am and the 'Hoff'. 1983 gave us The A-Team with explosions, stunts and no-one ever being shot and spilling any blood, despite the amount of bullets.

Buck Rogers in the 25th Century had however removed one of the basics that underpinned the franchise. The controller of BBC1, Alan Hart, had decided to move the show to a spring transmission as opposed to the usual winter transmissions. He also decided to swap it to two episodes per week, on a week night. This had the effect of halving the number of weeks the series was on-air to thirteen instead of twenty-six, as well as movement in the schedule.

This experiment in seeing the viability of running a twice-weekly drama serial would later lead to the launching of the massively popular soap opera, Eastenders in a similar slot. It also had the short-term effect of doubling the Doctor Who audience, (which had dramatically dropped to 5million in the last series), with the story Black Orchid being the final story of the regular run – and the only one of the 1980s – to break the double-figure millions barrier for the story overall, with a recorded figure of ten million viewers. The last individual episode with over ten million viewers was the first part of 1982's Time Flight.

The last two paragraphs seem to dispute my assertion that the shows producers were trying to go back to basics, when there were obviously making changes to the show right from the top. Well…some of the management wanted to strip it back to basics… some wanted to toy with it. And this would be a business lesson that would haunt the franchise for the next 8 years.

When things need to change you need everyone, and I mean everyone, on the same page. Otherwise some parts will work well, and others wont work so well. All in all, it will leave a business that is not performing as it should, holding itself back or be on a path to failure. Here at the very start of a tenure, the producers were doing lots of things, writers doing another, some actors doing something else and the suits at the top 'experimenting' with a show that had already seen a rapid decline. It's no different in business. One of the biggest rapid declines in a business in recent times has been the self-destruction of Toys R Us.

How can a chain of toy stores collapse? How can toys ever go out of fashion? Simple…you allow that management team somewhere near it. As you can tell, I'm a bit pissed at it.

Founded by Charles Lazarus in its modern iteration in June 1957, Toys "R" Us traced its origins to Lazarus's children's furniture store, which he started in 1948. He added toys to his offering, and eventually shifted his focus. The company had been in the toy business for more than 65 years and operated around 800 stores in the United States and around 800 outside the US, until it's untimely demise early in 2018. Toys "R" Us expanded as a chain, becoming predominant in its niche field of toy retail, and also branched out into baby supplies and children's clothing. At its peak, Toys "R" Us was considered a classic example of a 'category killer'. With the rise of mass merchants, as well as online retailers such as Amazon, Toys "R" Us began to lose its share of the toy market. And this is what the press and media wanted to talk about and have you believe that the 'landscape' had changed so much that it was forced to go out of business. Rubbish. Utter rubbish. It was, in my opinion some massive mistakes that embodied such a lack of leadership, that for a brand such as this to go belly up, should be looked upon as criminal. Be very, very careful when you hear the line 'It's moved to online' being trotted out. In 2018 for every £1 spent in retail, 84pence was spent in a bricks an mortar store. (ONS Figures December 2018)

It was at the start of the millennium the board decided to 'switch things up'. To improve the company, the board of directors installed John Eyler (formerly of FAO Schwarz) in May 2000. Eyler launched a very unsuccessful, expensive plan to remodel and re-launch the chain. Blaming market pressures (primarily competition from Walmart and Target), Toys "R" Us considered splitting its toy and baby businesses. The first issue here is that it is very easy, and I mean very easy to blame others as to why you are not doing well. It seems ridiculous now as we look back on the tatters of a business that was a business with such a reputation and affinity with peoples childhoods, that it find it easier to blame competition from 'pile it high sell it low' discounters. If this were the case, all the mid group and top quality retailers would also be out of business. It was because the strategy was wrong. Simple as.

It gets worse, on March 17, 2005, when a consortium of Bain Capital Partners LLC, Kohlberg Kravis Roberts (KKR) and Vornado Realty Trust announced a $6.6 billion leveraged buyout of the company. Public stock closed for the last time on July 21, 2005 at $26.74—a 63% increase since when it first announced that the company was put up for sale. Toys "R" Us became a privately owned entity after the buyout. Effectively it was saddled with a huge amount of debt and no genuine leadership team with a vision that was to became the straw that was to break Geoffrey the Giraffes back.

On August 23, 2011, Toys "R" Us announced it would begin to open combined Toys "R" Us/Babies "R" Us stores, with 21 new stores using the concept (11 of them having a full-sized "superstore" format), and 23 remodelled into the concept. In December 2013, eight days before Christmas, Toys "R" Us announced their stores in the United States would stay open for 87 hours straight. The flagship store of the retailer in Times Square was open for 24 hours a day from December 1 to December 24, to cater to tourists. The announcement came after snow and rain caused a nearly 9 percent year-over-year decline in U.S. store foot traffic. This move also pushed the retailer to hire an additional 45,000 seasonal workers to cater to the demand of the extended store hours. Since the toy business is incredibly seasonal, more than 40% of the company's sales come in during the fourth quarter of the year. It was a toy-train that was beginning to run out of control.

In 2014, Toys "R" Us announced its "TRU Transformation" strategy, which concentrated on efforts to fix foundational issues affecting future growth, including making stores less cluttered, improving the customer experience, clearer pricing strategies and promotions, and tighter integration of its retail and online businesses. In 2015, the company launched the first of a new concept store called the "Toy Lab" in Freehold, New Jersey. The new layout provided more space for interactive exhibits and areas to play with new toys before purchase. That concept was then expanded to stores in California, Delaware, Florida, New York and Pennsylvania. They were missing the boat. It was all too slow, too dated and no urgency.

On September 18, 2017, Toys "R" Us, Inc. filed for bankruptcy stating the move would give it flexibility to deal with it's $5 billion in long-term debt, borrow $2 billion so it could pay suppliers for the upcoming holiday season and invest in improving current operations. The staggering thing was that the company had not had an annual profit since 2013. It reported a net loss of US$164 million in the quarter ended April 29, 2017. It lost US$126 million in the same period in the prior year. It was an utter shambles and in early 2018 stores in the US and the UK closed their doors for the final time, and slowly across the rest of the world. The 'category killer' was now dead.

Had anyone gone shopping at Toys R Us in this last 10 years, they would simply tell you what the actual problems were. The management didn't change things fast enough. They made out-of-town stores 'destination stores' at a pace a snail would have been impressed with. The rest of the stores looked tired, cluttered and poorly staffed. However, Toys "R" Us may have 'broke itself' when it signed a 10-year contract to be the exclusive vendor of toys on Amazon in 2000. Amazon began to allow other toy vendors to sell on its site in spite of the deal, and Toys

"R" Us sued Amazon to end the agreement in 2004. As a result, Toys "R" Us missed the opportunity to develop its own e-commerce presence early on. It then went on to invest less than other vendors on their own online platform and by the time they went bust, were seeming to get it right with over 40% of their sales being online.

As you can see, it's very difficult to get 'restructuring' right and I'm happy to admit that. Whether it's going back to basics or trying to keep up, there is a common thread. It needs to be done with 'nimbleness'. I can only imagine the amount of meeting and counter meetings and final meetings that big business need to go through just to move a dot, comma or cross a 't'. This is where small business has a huge advantage and I mean a huge advantage. If you wanted to do something today; change a service, change your website, change your branding or stop selling something, you can do it within minutes or hours. You can move that quickly. Simple. So if you think something needs changing or you want to change something...change it. If you're waiting for permission, the only person you need to ask, is yourself.

Going back to the casting of Davison, some would say it was a master stroke. Popularity had declined in Baker's last year, because of various factors including the actor himself, the stories and its competition from flashy American imports. Every actor up until now, had a solid body of work behind them, but none were 'flavour of the month' or as 'busy' as Davison was. On our screens in 'All Creatures Great and Small', he was also in two other series called 'Sink or Swim' and 'Holding the Fort'. It was smart because the audience already knew him. It's downside? We effectively got the character from All Creatures Great and Small in a cricket outfit flying around space in a blue box. So I would suggest there would be another lesson here.

If you are going to launch or market a product or service that is already out there, but with a different look, make sure it has a different feel to the substance also. As humans we are very fickle beings, and we will quickly get over the fact that something looks a bit different and realise that we could have saved a few quid by sticking with something else, because it does nothing differently to the one we already have or is a few quid cheaper. Look at the issues that mobile phone developers are currently going through. Aesthetically they are all the same pretty much. The USP's are getting fewer and fewer. They're now a bit quicker and lighter and the cameras are almost as good as a professional camera. But once you get over that...nothing else really. So the 'hype' fades very quickly.

Davison himself has said that a serious discussion of how the character should be different from the other incarnations, never actually took place. The most serious discussion he had with the producer, (franchise leader), Jon Nathan-Turner, was what the Doctor should wear. The Fifth Doctor's chosen mode of dress was a variation of an Edwardian cricketers kit, and he was even seen to carry a cricket ball in one of his pockets (which saved his life in one adventure). He wore a cream-coloured frock coat, striped trousers, plimsoll shoes, and occasionally a pair of spectacles. He frequently wore an optimo-style Panama hat, that had a red band with a black and white pattern, which he would roll up and place in an inside coat pocket. It was all a bit 1980's and a bit 'meh' as we look back on it. And if you search the archives on YouTube, you'll actually find footage of an audience telling Davison how he should 'play' this incarnation of the Timelord or a programme called 'Pebble Mill at 1'. Someone in the production office thought this was a good idea. To be fair, it could be said that 'marketing and business gold' can be mined from your public, but this certainly wasn't the case here...because perhaps people were being asked the wrong questions. Ask the wrong questions, you'll get the wrong answers. Ask the right questions and you'll get the right answers, just not necessarily what you wanted to hear.

One of the things that hampered the start of this tenure and never really went away, was a problem in the production office. Nathan-Turner was not on the BBC books as a producer, even though he had been fulfilling the role for over 12 months. Then head of serials at the BBC, Graham McDonald was asked by the top brass to become 'Head of Series'. Which then meant he had twice as many programmes to deal with and no more resources. Although McDonald had given Nathan-Turner the role, he was not entirely convinced that he could cope and asked Barry Letts, a show veteran to step in and effectively do a Lead Executive Producers role on the show. Let's put it this way...it was like chalk and cheese. JNT was a flamboyant extrovert and Letts was the kind of bloke that would sit in the corner and think about things. Their opinions on the how the show should be run were quite simply not on the same wavelength from the start.

This just doesn't work when it comes to business, putting someone in to a role that has little or no connection with those already in a role. I've had it myself. Managers and Directors that have come in above me and wanted to change things because it's not what they would do. Even if something is working. In a minimal amount of cases you'll find that the experience they do have, actually helps you do your role. However, in a majority of situations, you'll often find that if there is little or no connection with the people they are there to manage, it's like a pushing wet spaghetti up-hill in a competition. It's just not going to work. Someone, somewhere is going to feel isolated and therefore work less efficiently and effectively. So at least wanting the same goals and having the same visions on how to get there are key to that type of relationship working.

The problem manifested itself in the form of disagreements on scripts. Letts would see things not making much sense, or not how they had previously done it on the show. Instead of JNT taking time to talk about it, he would brush Letts off and ask him to talk to the script editor. This meant he would often work late in to the night and even be locked in by the cleaning staff because he was changing so many things in the scripts. He moved on. The first part of collateral damage.

Antony Root joined the team as script editor and in his first meeting with JNT was given a pile of scripts and treatments that were deposited on his desk and was told which one was to be worked on first. At this point JNT told him he was off to America for a convention and he'd be back in a week. (Remember this was before emails and mobile phones!). In a parting shot, JNT said that if he really had to to speak to Letts, then speak to him.

The script that JNT had wanted to work on, and to be the opening episode of the new Doctor, was, in Root's own words, "Somewhere short of being able to be produced." This rookie was being asked to salvage something from a potential train-wreck. He should never have been put in this position. He went to Letts. He agreed.

Between them they found a script that was almost ready to be produced and finalised it. Told the director and the production team about what was to be done first and got on with it. When JNT came back there was a showdown. JNT had shirked responsibility and this goes further to prove what can happen when members of management have different views on how or what things need to be done. The series opener was hurriedly rewritten and changed in less than one week. And the rookie Root? A potential rough diamond? Left within a year. NOT how you treat new colleagues or members of your team.

Further to what I've already written, this goes to show what can happen to a team that has expectations and goals set by two different styles of management. It gets pulled apart and good people leave to do other things, because they don't want the added stresses, strains or hassles. If only senior managers were told what really happens when people don't get along...because one day they find out that they get low or no results, poor standards, a blame culture and poor morale amongst those that are left standing. And this is what was happening to the franchise.

Somehow, JNT was promoted to Producer full time and Letts agreed to step down after a year so that JNT could be sole producer of the show. Personally, I think this shows a huge amount of professional conduct by Letts as, whatever you read or see, you'll not find him being disparaging about what had happened. Letts went on to do some other fabulous things on the BBC and Dr Who was now the sole property of JNT. The fuse was now lit for it's demise.

Problems with scripts and quality of scripts continued. One of the 'going back to basics' had also caused yet another problem. The Tardis crew had grown to 4. The Doctor and three companions. Admittedly this was not a problem with Hartnell, because as his health faded, writers were able to give the companions more to do and even some episodes had no Doctor in them at all. But trying to give three companions enough to do and follow the Doctor was at best, 'clunky'. So a decision was made and it shocked Whovians all over the world. They killed off a companion. Adric, played by Matthew Waterhouse, was boy maths genius and unfortunately not the most likeable of characters. He met his death in a story called 'Earthshock', that had seen the much heralded return of the Cybermen, so it created a massive shockwave in the viewers when the companion 'heroically' died trying to save the human race. The series also ended with a cliff hanger as to whether one of the other companions, Tegan, had left the TARDIS. Despite the challenges that were going on behind the camera, the series, in the new time slot, with the new lead actor was a 'success'.

But how long do things behind the scenes, stay behind the scenes?

We touched on going back to basics and going back to the past. You can only do it for so long. Because of the praise and adulation from fans over the story with the returning Cybermen, 'Earthshock', JNT wanted more from the past. In fact there were returning monsters and villains in every episode of Davison's second season. Behind the scenes tensions were growing and now there were tensions between the main actor and the producer.

And this started boiling down to how the show was being marketed. It's been said that JNT was certainly the more flamboyant and extrovert of the producers of the show and he worked, without doubt at the beginning of his tenure to make Dr Who as marketable as possible. He would work exceptionally hard to get the show into the press, (remember no social media?!), as this would definitely have an effect on the ratings. He began to cast 'stars' into roles that would grab some media attention. Davison felt this was to the detriment of the show and in some cases the people that were cast weren't suitable for those roles when other talented actors could have played the part much better. It was the beginning of 'stunt' casting. Something that would lead to a massive split in opinions and mocking from some quarters. The 'stars' were mainly from the worlds of comedy and light entertainment with JNT himself saying numerous times, "...that there is very little difference between a comedy actor and a straight actor. It's just that short sighted people tend to pigeon-hole them as a comedy actor or a light entertainment star..."

He wanted to make the show larger than life and bigger in America. Admirable if not fool hardy at the time. Remember that the show had already taken a hell of a battering from imports on other channels. Publicity and marketing he thought, were his forte, so if he could generate interest by any means he would do. As some cast members have said, "If an actor in the show could get up on stage and do 'something', then it would benefit the show", with many having done 'cabaret style' performances in the US at conventions and promotional tours. His weakness was getting to grips with the drama and the sci-fi aspect of the show. His passion was variety and

Pantomime. So much so Davison was roped into doing a Pantomime in Tunbridge-Wells, that was also produced by JNT. Davison recounts at that time there was very little rehearsal of Dr Who, but more emphasis put on the Pantomime. Stunt casting, storylines not thought through, laughable effects, (even for it's time) and some poor acting meant that the significance of the show began to fall away.

A massive lesson here is not to let the quality of what you produce wain in the pursuit of other things.

As Nissa left the show, a new companion was bought in, Turlow...who's primary purpose was to 'kill the Doctor'. Well that may have been a good idea for a few episodes and after a bottle of white wine, but for a whole series? Awful.

Script writing descended into chaos. The show was becoming 'patchy'. Under previous production teams, the scripts had been more of a collaborative approach to writing. Under this team, some who had a passion for the show, shone. Others looked like they had been written in between jobs and lacked passion and any energy. The team approached writers to write for the show. If they were well known and the storyline was good, they would commission a script straight away. If they were inexperienced, they would ask for a scene break-down and of that was liked they would commission a script. In Eric Sayward's own words..."There was never much planning....". JNT was resistant, at old writers coming back. (Calling the legendary Robert Holmes, an "old fart"). It became apparent he knew very little about the scripting process, which was staggering given his number of years in the industry, yet he still wanted to keep full control of the whole process. Davison grew isolated as he didn't want to take sides and the writers, who essentially were in charge of the 'fictional world' in which the franchise inhabited were pushed well down the pecking order of importance when it came to decision making. What was forgotten, is that without good stories, there would be nothing to show. Without anything to show, there wouldn't be anything to market. It could be said that the show succeeded despite the 'managements' best efforts.

The cast and some of the production staff have gone on record also sighting that the directors used for the show, I guess in terms of this piece of work, the people managers, weren't the best. Many of them had just completed the directors course or they were old directors that were very experienced and just biding their time until a better job came along. They would then fall into two categories. The directors who did direct you and those that didn't direct you. Perhaps they should have come up with a better word than director then? But the same happens in management. Those that mange you and those who just...don't. (Until it all goes tits that is!) They are really what's known as facilitators. They get you into the right place, doing the right sort of thing to a point, but don't help you get better, or make the most of what you and the business has. It had become a 'workman-like' programme and the 'directors' were being asked to do a 'workman-like' job. Some would say based on it's budget they did well, but it really did show when someone with genuine passion came along and got every drop of drama or sci-fi out of an episode. You can't make a silk purse out of a sow's ear, but you could at least make practical bag!

Things came to a head when head writer Eric Sayward had a dispute with producer JNT about losing a very talented director. Sayward understanding that good directors were hard to come by, was appalled and dismayed when he realised that this one particular director had been dropped from the directors roster. JNT was now becoming a strutting peacock and would start and argument in an empty room. He had vast enthusiasm and this was his virtue. But it was masking his deficiencies. He was upsetting everyone and anyone, but would still get the show to the screen. He was in danger, (some say he ended up doing it anyway), of thinking he was bigger than the show he produced. Something that had been levelled at two of the actors in previous years.

Davison had become frustrated at the way the show was being run, the standard of writing and now the standards of directors for the shows. The viewers were also becoming frustrated. Viewing figures were beginning to slide and although they had not been treated entirely fairly with scheduling of this season, audiences started to feel there was something missing despite all of the crowd pleasing that was being attempted through casting and old foes. Add to this the beginnings of a new channel, Channel 4 and the rise of the home video recorder, maintaining viewing figures was getting harder than ever. It needed to change. Again.

There was some brief respite and salvation on the way. A 20th Anniversary of the show was on it's way. The stakes were high. Five Doctors, countless companions and even more aliens this was due to be a celebration of the highest order. But this threw up more bumps than was really needed. Despite his own rule of not going back to old writers, Robert Holmes was asked to write a script, however he found the shopping list of what was allowed and what wasn't allowed creatively stifling. So it fell to another 'old fart' in the form of Terence Dicks to pull a script together. Another bump came in the form of Tom Baker not wishing to reprise his role so soon after giving up his tenure and trying to move away from the type-casting he was experiencing. The next was a re-casting of the first Doctor with Richard Hurndall taking up the role that had been played by William Hartnell. Some loved it, some hated it. I fell into the later camp if I'm honest. The show did draw some media attention to the viewing public that the franchise was still there and I guess for it's time, wasn't as bad as we think it is now. But having grown so unhappy with what happened over the last twelve months, Davison informed JNT that his next series would be his last, having been offered an option to go for a fourth series. (Although how much truth there is in that is debatable. Patrick Troughton, (the 2nd Doctor), is often lauded as the man that told Davison to go, suggesting that anymore than three series would mean he ran the danger of being type-cast. Davison says it was because of his experience on the second season that he based his decision.)

Alongside the special, BBC Enterprises chose to do their own version of Dr Who 'Woodstock' which gave them an insight into how popular the show could be and embarrassingly how it should have been. There was an official two-day convention held at Long-Leat House in Wiltshire. There were all four living Doctors there, including Tom Baker, as well as sets, monsters, props, make-up, panels and merchandise. I said embarrassingly earlier as BBC Enterprises, (despite JNT's protestations....something he did get right!), only expected a few thousand to visit. Over 40,000 people visited in a two day period, long before things such as comic-con and TV and Movie shows. Many left disappointed, but although Davison wasn't 'seen' to be as big a personality as at least a couple of his predecessors, he spent all of his scant free time walking up and down the long queues signing autographs and shaking hands with fans of the show. These mistakes when it came to publicity and merchandising would not happen under the new series running at present.

I guess the lessons to be learned from here is to not underestimate what your public really wants and what they are prepared to pay for. The 'surprise' came here from people who hadn't pre-booked tickets and in a world in which live nowadays, I doubt this would happen again. I can't imagine Wembley allowing anyone to turn up. But with the right amount of promotion and marketing a business needs to also be able to 'manage' it's customers expectations. If you have a limited space or quantity of something, then manage that expectation. There is always going to be some disappointment somewhere, but learn from those mistakes and make incremental changes. Retailers historically are pretty crap at this in general. They have something on sale at 'X' amount and because they have sold 100 units in a day, order a 1000 units and have 950 sat on the shelf for the rest of the year. I saw this with a firm that imports Halal

Cola and Orangeade. They sold a bucket load to retailers and shopkeepers up and down the country. And because they'd sold an entire container in less than a month they ordered more. A lot more. I walked in when they still had 4 containers left from 4 containers ordered, six months after their initial selling spree. The product was good and in a blind taste test, you'd struggle to put it below premium, well known products. But it just didn't sell in the stores. There was little or no brand awareness and it just sat on people's shelves waiting to be discounted. Wait for feedback on wether something is a hit or not. Do research. Being 'oversubscribed' is not a bad thing and can be a cause for celebration and maybe price increases. It may also be down to the fact you have misread the marketplace. On the flip side, just because you sold a quantity of a product or service in one hit, may not mean the market is as big as you think it is when it comes to doing it a second time.

The scripts deliberately tried to go darker for the next series to recapture the haemorrhaging viewership, but some of the special effects were now laughable. In one story there was a monster that was so rubber, and slow, you can actually see the cast smirking at the 'threat' that was being posed. They tried to recapture some form in all the chaos with the Master and the Daleks returning. Some fans thought it had gone back to Davison's first series levels but the decision had already been made. In fact, three decisions had been made. Mark Strickland, (Turlow) and Janet Fielding, (Tegan) had also decided to leave. It was a full character changing of the guard. (Fielding reportedly hated the whole thing so much she actually gave up acting! Wow!) And in a break from recent tradition, Nathan-Turner decided to regenerate the Doctor in the season's penultimate story, to introduce the Sixth Doctor to audiences before the seasonal break. Davison's last regular appearance as the Fifth Doctor was in the last episode of The Caves of Androzani by 'old fart' Robert Holmes, broadcast on 16 March 1984.

Davison returned to the role briefly in the 1993 awful charity special Dimensions in Time. Then beginning in 1999, he recorded a series of *Doctor Who* radio dramas for Big Finish Productions. In 2007, Davison, at the age of 56, appeared alongside the Tenth Doctor, David Tennant in a *Doctor Who* special for the charity Children in Need, written by then show-runner Steven Moffat and titled "Time Crash". This was the first official time that a Doctor from the new series met a Doctor from the original 26-year run.

He was and should have been, my Doctor. He did something that many thought difficult. He slipped in the space left by Tom Baker. He captured new hearts and new minds of children who have grown up to love Dr Who. Most importantly, he helped mould the hearts and minds of the writers and show-runners that run the franchise right now. Not a bad legacy when chaos was reigning all around him...but for now the seeds of things to come had been planted and we're in for a bumpy ride!

So things we've learned from the Fifth Doctors time:

1. **Going back to the past is only where SOME of the answers are**. It fixes certain things for some people. You see, life and business evolve. Different generations want different things and do different things different ways. The Baby-Boomers want different things to the Millenials, yet we all operate in the same market place and your goods or services could be as useful to me or my 16 year old son. Take the good of the past, and lace it into the new. That means it has connection and relevance.

2. **Experiment with new things, but not to the detriment of the original product**. In this scenario, there was too much experimentation. Storylines, days and times when the episodes were being shown, etc. It effected the show going forward, (more of that to come). But if you take a look at the failure of 'New Flavour Coke', which was launched in April 1985, experimenting can have devastating effects on your business. Launched as a replacement for the original flavouring, it was pulled from the shelves quickly when sales fell off a cliff. People just didn't enjoy

it and it was too far removed from what people had been used to. Right now they seem to have it right. You can have original tasting Coke, but you can also have Peach, Mango, Vanilla, Cherry, Sugar Free, Caffeine Free, etc, etc...but it's the customers choice as to what they have. Just replacing a well known option with something relatively untried, (yes, I'm sure they did do taste tests, but that's not a true representation of the millions of bottles and cans sold around the world), is a suicidal business decision.

3. **Get everyone on the same page when changes happen**. I've described the rise and fall of Toy's R Us in this chapter and part of the failure was not to be quick and nimble as it could or should have been. As a small business, you can change as quick as you want or need. Don't be afraid of it. It's a strength. Ask peoples opinions, preferably those of your customers and of people that you respect and implement what you need to do at pace. It could be the difference between you going backwards or moving onwards and upwards.

4. **If you're going to employ someone or put someone in place to work with a team, make sure there is a connection between them**. In business opposites very rarely attract. They usually lead to low deliverables, failure and infighting. And usually by the time you've realised it, it's too late. People must be on the same page, with same vision and same goals. Add to that

similar working methods and values. Otherwise you may need to make a decision about the people already in place...are they right for what you want in your business? You cannot run a business by democracy, a leader needs to emerge and be followed.

5. **Is the line of management or decision makers within your business the right one?** Taking this period of the franchises history, it could be argued that the writers were pushed far too far down the production structure. The writers are, as show-runner Stephen Moffat says, are 'in charge' of the fictitious world in which the franchise inhabits. So do the right people have the right amount of say in your business and help you understand it's direction?

6. **Substance over image**. Getting something in or someone in to promote a service or product is fine, providing it gives the value that's being tantalised. With this Doctor we ended up getting an out-of-breath floppy haired vet in space. A shame as the writing, effects and casting did nothing to back up the promise of a new young Doctor. Always do things with value and the customer in mind. It's not all about you...there's a bigger picture that always needs to be addressed.

7. **Manage peoples expectations and manage your own at the same time**. Wait for feedback. Wait to see whether there is an appetite for what you want to offer at the price you want to offer it.

Don't screw something that works well, when you can experiment with things by ADDING value to original products or services. Ask the right questions, looking for uncomfortable answers.

# The Sixth Doctor

So here we are. 16th March 1984 and Colin Baker sits bolt upright staring straight into the camera and says, "Change my dear…and not a moment too soon." Well it was certainly to be a change. Thirty four months of being the Doctor, with 18 of them being on 'hiatus', violence, media storms, very public arguments and apologies and lessons in how NOT to do things. This was the Sixth Doctor and this was a lesson in how to wreck a franchise.

Earlier I spoke of how Gerald Ratner managed to wreck a business with one speech. It was painful, showed a lack of thought and a lack of respect to a customer base that had spent hard-earned money with him. Well here we have the equivalent over a 34 month period that would wreck a franchise for a very long time, and would take years and a generation to right the wrongs.

The Sixth Doctor appeared in three seasons. His appearance in the first of these was at the end of the final episode of The Caves of Androzani, which featured the regeneration from Peter Davison's Doctor. It was a change to convention and a proven formula in that the regeneration was not at the end of a season. It was the penultimate story of the seasons run. The following week he appeared in the final story of the season 'The Twin Dilemma", and this is where the problems began.

The Sixth Doctor's regeneration was initially unstable, and he nearly strangled his companion Peri before he came to his senses. It was a frightening scene and something of which Dr Who fans had never seen before. In many scenes he appeared to be going mad and his costume was utterly horrendous, even for the 1980's. Add to that a poor story where guest actors were utterly wooden, this NEW Doctor left a taste in the mouth like drinking white wine vinegar. It may say 'white wine', but it's still vinegar. As far as 'launches' go…this was the worst possible start as it wasn't until the beginning of January, the following year, that we would see the character again. As fans and viewers of the show, we were left with a Doctor that has tried to kill his companion, was mentally unstable, quite unlikable, arrogant and a bloody awful story to go out on.

Our first lesson here, is that whilst we deal with change well as a species, we cant deal with that much change, that fast, and that drastic. It's like Harrods shutting down and reopening with Primark stock to sell instead. It doesn't make a lot of sense and would alienate all those people who spend hundreds of pounds on a pair of socks instead of £6 for a pack of 5 pairs.

If this introduction of such a contrasting personality had been the first episode of the next full series, then there was going to be scope for a story arc to show why he was that way and see where would it would lead. Instead what the public got was the reveal of something they thought they knew, but in fact was absolutely nothing like they remembered. It was a bad start. In business networking and marketing, you have roughly seven, yes, seven seconds to make a good impression. There are different situations when making a first impression counts, but let's start with the most traditional: meeting someone in person, whether it's in a client meeting or at a networking event.

Dress and groom appropriately.

This should go without saying, but people will judge you on your looks long before they judge your words or actions. After all, it only takes a fraction of a second to start making snap judgments, and we do it all the time. It's no problem for us to imagine that we understand why a person has taken a particular course of action or is the way they are. We actually don't really know; we make a guess based on our imagination, past experiences or even wishful thinking.

In all our perceptions, from vision to hearing, to the pictures we build of a persons character, our unconscious mind starts from whatever objective data there is available to us – which is usually patchy and instant at best – and helps to shape and construct the more complete picture we consciously perceive.

In order to offer us this more complete picture, our unconscious employs some clever tricks and educated guesses to fill in some blanks. In our perception of people, and their perceptions of us, the hidden, subliminal mind takes limited data, and creates a picture that seems clear and real, but is actually built largely on unconscious inferences that are made, employing factors such as a person's body language, their voice, (but not what they are actually saying), clothing, appearance, and social category.

Thus, you should start off on the right foot by dressing appropriately for an event, interview or meeting. This certainly wasn't good news for the new lead actor and face of the franchise, which I'll come on to later. While we all may wish there weren't expectations placed on our appearance in terms of professional events, the reality is that they are; small things like hair and makeup can actually nudge people to see you as more influential. wearing more casual attire rather than a suit and shiny shoes, may make people perceive you as less professional.

Smiling is shown to be a psychological signal of altruism (among other positive signs). When you smile at someone, it makes someone more likely to trust you, and it makes you seem more approachable. Flashing a smile in those first seven seconds of meeting someone may be all it takes to forge a stronger first impression and connection. So can you imagine a face of a franchise looking angry and acting like they were having an utter breakdown resulting in violence against a female companion. Bloody hell. This was going to take some coming back from. First impressions count; always have and always will. To forget this rule is a tragic way to lose business and damage your brand.

To further this continuation with how things looked, this Doctor's legacy could well be summed up by the utter mess he was expected to dress as. Mocked by many, hated by more, the characters sense of style completely went out of the window. The actor himself, Colin Baker wanted to dress his Doctor in black velvet, to reflect his character's darker personality. Which judging by the first episode would have made sense. The franchise top-dog, Producer John Nathan-Turner however, opted for a deliberately "totally tasteless" costume with clashing colours. Designer Pat Godfrey made several attempts which were considered 'not tasteless enough' before JNT finally accepted the last one as sufficiently garish. Colin Baker later described the outfit as "an explosion in a rainbow factory", which at best is an understatement.

The Sixth Doctor wears a red plaid frock coat, with green patchwork, and yellow and pink lapels over a white shirt with red question marks embroidered in the collar (a feature of the programme since 1980), a waistcoat and large Victorian style necktie, and yellow trousers with black stripes and a pair of green ankle boots with red spats. There were many variants on the waistcoat and tie, the earliest being the knitted brown waistcoat and turquoise polka-dot tie. The waistcoat was later changed to red check, and in the following story a new red polka-dot tie appeared. The "future" version of the Sixth Doctor seen aboard the

*Hyperion III* (*The Trial of a Time Lord*) wore a striped waistcoat and a yellow tie speckled with black stars. Baker added a cat badge to the ensemble. It was horrendous. Was this a reflection of the times? Barely. Was this a sign of who the Doctor was? Hardly. Was this a reflection of the real leader of the franchise? Maybe.

There were many fans, critics and people who 'knew stuff' that have said that the attire and image of this version of the character was JNT putting himself in the role of the Doctor without ever appearing on screen. He was the flamboyant, PR driven producer and yet the character was a dark, brooding and unlikeable version of himself so the costume and over the top dress sense just never ever sat right. It would be like your mobile phone brand suddenly bringing out a new phone shaped like a pig. Just plainly weird, not wanted and not practical. It was yet another decision by the franchise leader that was bewildering.

But now it gets darker and even weirder as a power struggle began to develop that saw a show being pulled apart and messed about. Baker's first series had a top viewership of 8.9 million for the first episode of the series, and a low of 6 million. In one way you could look at it that it had 'lost' 2.9 million viewers, but the lows were actually half way through the series and by the end of its last episode was watched by 7.7

million, so they recovered to lose only 1.2 million. Statistics like this were difficult to quantify, because of video recordings, etc, at the time, so it was likely that it could have been more. The nature of it's 'up and down' script writing quality didn't help as well as fair-weather viewers acknowledgment of its it poor effects thanks to the previous five years. It's tags of wobbly sets and rubber monsters were hard to lose. Add to that the 'ramping up' of the perceived violence in the show, this would start getting protestors like Mary Whitehouse asking for it to be banned or put on after 9pm; the 'watershed' time on TV.

We also got a change to the format AGAIN. It moved from it's midweek slots back to a Saturday tea-time slot, which meant that it was to be aired 1hr and 20 minutes earlier than it had been under Davison's Doctor, and then head of BBC1, Alan Hart, decreed that the episodes would be double the length they had been with the 5th Doctor. This meant there would be a halving of the number of episodes from 26 to 13. There were cost implications, because halving the episodes and doubling the time on screen of those episodes, would result in an extra 50 minutes of production needed for the series, because recaps and titles were no longer being used to fill the run times. So Hart was finally convinced to reduce the run time down to 45 minutes, instead of 50 minutes.

From a narrative point of view, unfortunately the writers didn't adapt, and tried to follow what had worked with previous series. The first episode being the set up with the villain of the story being revealed at the end. Then the adventure unfolds. Unfortunately this structure is stretched out so you end up having a 25 minute episode, 'padded' to 45 minutes.

When it comes to business lessons, changing for the sake of changing is never a good thing. As you're reading this I bet somewhere at home you a favourite something. A jumper, pair of slippers, seat on the sofa, or set of pants. There is something just really pleasant about them always being there and we find it comforting. The fact that the show had been playing the 'hokey-cokey' on the schedule was unsettling for the team and for it's viewers. As I've said before, people like certainty. By changing it, they were now changing the structure of the end product. There had to be some give and take, and although on the face of it, we were getting twice the show in one hit, we were getting less quality in value because the writers couldn't adapt. It had become watered down and offering customers and clients something that is watered down is a path to a worrying failure.

In some cases you could argue that when companies do this, it's called 'shrinkflation' and this is a real thing. Every year products and services are looked at to see if a product shrinks in size but its price doesn't. The Office for National Statistics (ONS), studied the price of 17,000 items between September 2015 and June 2017. It found 206 products in all categories had shrunk in size, while 79 increased.

Among bread and cereals the ONS found 36 cases of shrinkflation. The next two categories with the largest number of shrinkflation cases were meat and confectionery.. So things like your Jaffa Cakes, Toblerone and Hobnob Biscuits have all shrunk in size.

But most categories also saw some products increase in size. There were 18 increases in size among the bread and cereal category, and 13 meat products where this happened.

The category most likely to rise in size for the same price was tobacco, where there were also no examples of packets shrinking.

Shrinkflation is not a widespread problem, although products are much more likely to contract than expand. The ONS estimates that in 2016, just 1-2.1% of food products in its sample shrunk in size, while 0.3-0.7% got bigger. Over the last few years, consumers will have noticed that some companies have reduced the size of their products while the price remained the same, which is often attributed to operational and material cost rises. And in the past, companies blamed the rising price of raw materials. However, in the last couple of years these prices dropped back, but the shrinkage has continued. The ONS went onto investigate whether this was due to the fall in the pound, but said it hadn't spotted trends that can be attributed to a 'Brexit effect'. It may simply be that manufacturers have found a way to boost their profits under the radar.

The public aren't stupid. Messing your customers or clients around and expecting them to accept a substandard, watered down or stretched product or service just won't wash. You should always increase the value of a product or service so that your customers clients don't grow away. Improve a formula. Improve it's life expectancy. Add more freebies on it. Just try not to water it down.

Power struggles behind the scenes spilled out once more on to the screen, (it was becoming a real 'thing' under JNT's leadership), as script editor Eric Seyward, who was still peeved at the decision not to consult him about who was going to be the new Doctor, made sure that scripts 'sidelined' the Doctor and spent more time concentrating on scenario's and other characters than the Doctor himself. You could say, arguably, this was sabotage from within. This was unfair on the lead actor, and as the 'face of the franchise', would always bare the brunt of any viewer backlash that was to be unleashed. A bad workman always blames his tools. But a good workman makes the best of the tools he has, and in Baker's case, I think he did his best, with what he was given. If Seyward had personal misgivings, he should have got over them. If he felt his position was untenable, he should have moved on. If there was a difference in vision and strategy, no matter how you look at it, Seyward worked for JNT and not the other way round.

Now this is awkward. Especially when you have two people in the business that think they know what's right and what's wrong. Someone somewhere is going to have to take a decision and take the lead.

You have enough to deal with as the supervisor or boss at your workplace - but when someone's trying to sabotage you, it's time to drop a few things off the list and give the issue the attention it deserves. An employee who's trying to sabotage you or your company is a big problem that could result in reduced productivity, a damaged company reputation or a spread of the virus that results in total mutiny. Minimise the damage by taking action now.

Develop a workplace code of conduct, and put it in your employee handbook. By clearly outlining the behaviours that are accepted and not accepted in the workplace, you'll have something to refer to when an employee gets out of line. Your code of conduct code may include directions about what employees can and cannot reveal about the company in social media and other outside outlets, how they deal with the press, and how employees are expected to treat one another. Make all employees aware that you've created this code of conduct; or if you already have one, send it out as a reminder.

Open up the lines of communication. If you have one employee who's trying to sabotage you, chances are they have some complaints - and they may not be the only one. Allow the employee to sound off about their complaints in a group setting, such as a regularly scheduled team meeting in which all staff are invited to make suggestions for improving the workplace. During these meetings, be very careful in your language and communication materials, taking steps to show workers that you want their voices to be heard. When you hear feedback, work on implementing the suggested changes, and then report back about your progress at the next meeting.

Document any instances of sabotage you observe. If you already know the employee is trying to sabotage you, chances are it's because you've seen or heard about things she's doing to bring you down. Write down the date, time and nature of the incidents, and keep them in a safe place where co-workers will not stumble upon them. In the event that the problem escalates and the employee tries to get you fired -- or tries to destroy the reputation of the company -- you'll have evidence of her directed efforts against you, which may prove she's more vindictive than victim.

Arrange a one-on-one meeting, (no matter how painful it may feel), with the employee to discuss the issues they may be having. Sometimes, simply talking about the issues may help you discover what it is about you that the employee doesn't like. This may involve developing an action plan for both you and them to follow, so that you're both engaging in behaviours that are amenable to both parties. By remaining humble and listening to what they have to say, you may be able to come to some compromise that has them feeling listened to and understood, while at the same time leaving you feeling more secure about the future. At the same time, remember that you're the boss; so remain the authority and don't let her dictate all the terms. After the meeting, document the content of the conversation.

If all else fails, talk with a Human Resources expert about the problem. If things are getting out of hand and you've made an attempt to solve the issue yourself, you need to get others involved. Your HR expert can help you monitor the situation and keep an eye out for bad behaviour; they can also provide direction about a possible reassignment of duties for the person, or possibly even advise that you let the person go.

Once again old foes returned. Cybermen, The Master and The Daleks. It would seem that people were short on ideas and that going back to fan favourites seemed the best way to do things. But in amongst these typical, formulaic retreads was a hidden gem in the form of a story that was a satire on modern life in the 1980's, called Vengeance on Varos. To me it was a commentary on how TV and life was changing with people being executed on the vote of a watching public. (Way before X factor ever appeared!) Sighted by many critics as how the franchise had become too violent for it's ideal market, it was actually a parody of how TV had become a place for humiliation as entertainment. It was also a commentary on how there was a resurgence in people wanting the return of capital punishment and the cain in schools for people to 'tow the line' in society. Another source of inspiration for this story was the moral panic amongst certain sections of the public because of so-called 'video nasties', due to the rise of the affordable video machine. Strangely these were the same people that were slamming the show, even though they had been trying to make a commentary about how right they were when it came to the 'video nasty' material.

One of the things I advocate whole heartedly is be authentic and have an opinion. The stories at this time were reflecting a changing time, rightly or wrongly. But through the medium of the franchise it could be said that the wider organisation, the BBC were showing their feelings to what was happening. As a rule the BBC is meant to stay impartial, so in theory it can never say someone is right or wrong, but it can and still does reflect a certain amount feeling towards a subject matter. In business this is not a crime. In fact I think you should welcome it, because it will attract the right customers for you and your brand. If you are a business that has a very ecological mindset and is based around recycling of products then when something comes to the attention of the public you absolutely should have a say on it. Because the public you will engage with through these conversations are your ideal customers and client.  Think of the fair-trade movement in coffee and coca. When certain places launched that they were part of it because they believed in it, customers followed them in their droves.

But would it also interest you to know that some of those same businesses originally din't have that opinion?

I strongly believe that the best ideas and the right opinions for a business to take arise out of group discussions and a group mentality with its staff or it's customers. A single individual may have a great idea, but that idea will almost always be better - and stronger - when it has been debated, tested and fleshed out by a group of people. It then becomes the group's decision, and will be all the stronger because everyone buys into it.

But getting a group of employees or customers to come to a unanimous  agreement is not always easy. When people get together to talk over an issue, simple things will often take the meeting off the rails. I see it all the time in large and small businesses. From board meetings to Mastermind Group Coaching. And if you still don't believe me, do Jury Service and see what happens there.

Here, from my own experience, are tips for keeping discussions focused on outcomes - and preventing egos from scuttling the meeting.

1.  **Be inclusive and make sure to involve people who have an interest and opinion on the outcome.**

Don't exclude people you know should be present - it's a short-sighted tactic. What you want is a meaningful discussion where input can be presented on a level playing field at the right time. And the best way to have a rich discussion is to tap into the right opinions and perspectives.

Establish context and goals. Suppose you're building a house. You can't hold a meeting to discuss how many bathrooms the house should contain once construction has started. The time to have that meeting is when the house is still in the design stage. So if you are organising a meeting, make sure the timing is right. When it comes to an opinion don't announce it first, then have a meeting about it, otherwise it maybe a 'foot-in-mouth' moment.

You should also make it clear - in advance - what a meeting's goals are and what outcomes you are expecting. To use the house analogy again, if the meeting is about how many bathrooms the house should have, it should not end up in a discussion about which contractor to hire. Defining the topic and expected outcomes in advance will help keep the meeting focused.

## 2. At the meeting: Make sure participants are comfortable giving their own opinions.

Participants in the meeting should not feel intimidated or inhibited. They should feel they can express

themselves fully, and you should make it clear they are free to do so. Assume positive intent: If you've asked them to the meeting, assume they want to contribute to the discussion, not torpedo it.
If you see participants digging in their heels, or heating up emotionally, it's important to have a few strategies in your back pocket to focus the talks.

For example, you may be able to calm a frustrated participant by asking that person to help you understand their point of view. Or if one issue is causing tempers to flare, you can ask that the discussion on that topic be paused and move on to something else for a while (as long as you do get back to the topic).

## 3. Listen!

I know…bloody obvious right? It's really important to listen to what people say. Often, that's hard to do. Something a participant says may give you a flash of insight, and all you can think of is getting your idea out.
Keep yourself in check. Let the speaker finish - and listen to what they are saying.

Listening also means determining whether the meeting is moving towards an agreement - or whether participants are going off on a tangent.

## 4. Keep an open mind.

Don't hold a discussion to rubber-stamp a decision that has already been made. You have to be open to new ideas and new ways of doing things – even if they upset your original thoughts.

I'd want everyone to come to the meeting with an opinion, but that does not mean I want them to leave with the same opinion. As American marketing specialist Guy Kawasaki has said: "Smart people change their minds. It's dumb people who don't."

At this point in time, the franchise really had started to lose its way and it's key principals. To try something different they even bought back the Sontarans, the Second Doctor and his companion Jamie with location shooting in Seville. It was a bloated, padded out story with 'stuff' shoe-horned in and the location wasn't even necessary to the plot. It was perhaps a stunt too many for fans. But despite the worrying production issues, the first season of Colin Baker's Doctor actually finished with reasonably good ratings. The series finished with a story featuring the 'timeless' Daleks, but changes behind the scenes would mean more trouble fro the franchise.

The Sixth Doctor's era was marked by the decision of the BBC controller Michael Grade to put the series on an 18-month "hiatus" between seasons 22 and 23. Grade has been on record, even as he started the role, as saying he hated sci-fi (or anything HE didn't rate as quality television or had massive ratings). He cancelled the John Christophers adaptation of the Tripods and even wanted to cancel the comedy Blackadder after it's first season, (can you think of that now looking back.) So Dr Who was in his crosshairs.

When it came to cuts in programming because of a 'financial crisis' in the BBC, and the anticipated cost of the launch of the seminal soap opera Eastenders, with 104 episodes ordered for it's first year, the public and the press learned of the canceling of the franchise. Grade had underestimated the backlash that followed. With the press and fans having a full on, public outcry. He thought the public would have accepted this with little or no fuss because he believed that the public had grown 'tired' of this long running show. In his mind it had, had it's day as it was being overshadowed by it's flashy and glitzy American imports. To combat this they tried to justify the decision with several reasons being given and some that would contradict each other. The show was too violent…it had lost its appeal…the production team were no longer striving for excellence…the 45 minute episode experiment had failed and a rethink was needed. The press and the public wouldn't let up and this led to one of the most embarrassing and humiliating bits of memorabilia to be ever developed. A 'record', or 'single' as they were known then, called 'Doctor in Distress' was commissioned by someone to help bring Doctor back to our TV's whilst raising money for Cancer Relief. It was absolutely one of the worst records and songs of all time. Shocking. Just shocking. Z minus celebrities and singers and as good as actress Doctor Who companion Nicola Bryant was, she simply can't hold a note in a bucket. Just horrible. But despite this unintentional event of trying to destroy the dignity of the franchise, Grade and BBC1 controller Jonathan Powell were suitably persuaded by the backlash to reassure the public it would return after an 18 month hiatus.

**Your lesson for this is very, very, very simple.** Listen to your customer base. In this scenario the new head of the BBC just walked in and decided without consultation that the franchise should be killed off because it was not his cup-of-tea. He was wrong. Ford may not like selling the Ford Ka, and prefer it if I bought a Mustang, but the reality is that they realise that I can't afford nor have any need for a Mustang, so then I have the option of the Ka.

If you are in position of power, one of the most important things you can do at the start of, and throughout your journey is to talk to and listen to your customers. They have the best ideas. They have the answers you are looking for. It made no sense to get rid of a show that still pulled in 7 million viewers on a Saturday tea-time. What would you replace that product or service with? Don't just assume they will then buy whatever you are offering as a replacement as many will feel so undervalued, they will just go elsewhere. Don't risk it. Ask them what they want and wether there are better ways of doing things to get the same end result, which in this case was to reduce it's financial commitments. You haven't always got the right answers, sometimes opening yourself up to others opinions is the biggest step towards finding them and getting even better ones than you dreamed of.

The production team moved away from it's previous plans for the show in favour of a season long story arc which would link the different episodes. Seyward came up with the idea of the Doctor being on trial, more, in his won words out of desperation rather than any creativity. Art was about to reflect reality as many thought this was to be the last throw of the dice.

The format changed yet again, returning to a 25 minute run time and with only 14 episodes commissioned. A run that meant that this was now a series cut in half compared to previous years. It upset the public, again.

The season took the format of three, four part stories, set in the past, the present and the future, with the last two episodes destined to tie up the trail at the end. However Robert Holmes, the writer of the last two episodes died after a short illness only completing one of the scripts. Now in an unenviable position of having to complete the last episode himself, his relationship with JNT virtually broken and feeling guilty about his part in 'pushing the writer towards an early death', Eric Seyward quit with immediate effect, withdrawing the use of his script after what he considered silly and ill-advised feedback from the script he had written. It was now an absolute mess and things hung finely in the balance. At his wits end JNT summoned a husband and wife writing team to craft a suitable conclusion with only the previous script as guidance. He was not even allowed to advise on what had been in Seyward's script as a lawyer was present at all times during this experience, so much had the JNT and Seyward relationship relationship broken down. This was so that his intellectual property was not infringed upon. Sets had been constructed and actors booked, so the team of Pip and Jane Baker had only three days in which to connect the dots and write a script that was watchable.

The season was not the success that the public had wanted, but was at least 14 more episodes of a

British Institution. It was notably more lightweight and calmer than the season that proceeded it. With a toning down of the violence, the increase in humour and lightening of the colours. It was the work of a franchise under fire and there was a sharp drop in ratings by about 2 million per episode but it bought itself a pardon from Michael Grade.

JNT was then given an ultimatum. As he picked up the phone to his personally chosen star and Doctor, he had a choice between the franchise itself and backing the incumbent face of the same franchise. As Baker answered, he said "I've got some good news… and some bad news…"

So let's recap on the lessons from the short, but very, very turbulent Sixth Doctor's reign:

1. Unlike a TV franchise, **we have exactly 7 seconds in which to make a good impression**. It almost doesn't matter what we say, because of other people's experiences, prejudices and dispositions we are wired to make assumptions about the other person or even business after 7 seconds. So what can you do to make those 7 seconds count? What can you do to your physical or property appearance to make the most positive impression?

2. **Don't water stuff down just because of the cost implications**. Always try to ADD value wherever possible as your public aren't stupid and they will always work out what's better value for them sooner rather than later.

3. **If you see someone in the business sabotaging the business, do something about it**. Don't let it linger. By ignoring it and putting your head in the sand, it will do more harm than good. Nip it in the bud and decide what to do going forward.

4. **Yes have an opinion, but don't be afraid to change it**. Your customers and clients have opinions and they will be attracted to you and your business because of yours. If you run a larger business take a census of what the opinion should be and work from that basis. You are not going to please everyone, but the last thing you want is to have a mass walk out of customers and staff because you publicly oppose everything that your company has ever stood for. Listen to what's really going and be as educated as you can be to be able to form an opinion…not just repeating your mate Dave from down the pub.

5. **Ask the questions of your customers**. Out there right now is someone with the answer to the one thing that is holding your business back. Invite different opinions, thoughts and perspectives on a problem. Making a rash

decision can comeback to haunt you and it may take some time to get people back through your doors or buying your services if to everyone else, it was the wrong decision in the first place.

6. **Well**...I've got some good news and some bad news...it's definitely a lesson but it'll be at the start of the next chapter...

## The Seventh Doctor

"Colin, I've got got news and bad news. The good news is that the series is coming back."
"What's the bad news?"
"You're not..."

That was how (in dramatic terms), Colin Baker was let go as the the face of the franchise.

You have to feel for the guy big time. Rubbish stories, unrest behind the scenes, disinterest of the entire franchise from above, you can't help but feel that Colin Baker was made a scapegoat for a lot of people that shouldn't have been in charge. But here's the real kicker, he was asked to commit to a rough date of March the following year to film his last episodes so he could regenerate as others before him had. This meant it would have been near impossible for the actor to commit to any other work that he was offered. Quite rightly, after the shoddiness of his treatment, he declined to reappear. You could hardly blame him.

Add to that a newspaper article where he called the top man at the BBC, Michael Grade a coward and had many of his comments taken out of context, it would also prove to make sure he was never asked again. I guess if you're going to go make sure the rides that bind you are well and truly cut.

Here's our first lesson from the McCoy area, and he hasn't even appeared yet. The 'sacking' or 'removal' of the face franchise was being done very publicly. It's not the done thing in business, and rarely provides good vibes toward a business moving forwards. (Unless you are a soccer manager of course). Back then it was done by media and press, and nowadays it can be done even easier, in real time and with added viciousness with social media. Now I'm all for the right to reply, especially if someone has come out and publicly attacked you, but where there is distinct acrimony, it's better left behind closed doors and that will show some class.

Public criticism tends to leave stain on everybody involved. No-one comes out of this well. Two sides to every story and all that. It would be fair to say that Baker didn't come out of this well, but to the real core of fandom, it was always acknowledged that he got a raw deal. The science of hindsight is probably the most exact science in the world and given time opinions change.

As for using that right of reply, I'm going to refer you to an edition of Gordon Ramsay's 'Kitchen Nightmares'. The episode first aired on 2013 and centred on Ramsay attempting to help Amy and Samy Bouzaglo, owners of Amy's Baking Company in Arizona. The episode actually marked the only time in the series that the owners prevented Ramsay from completing the restaurant's transformation. The owners' behaviours received negative attention on social media, and the manner in which they responded to this critical reception further fuelled the controversy, prompting Forbes Magazine to refer to this as an example of how a business should not react to comments posted on social media.

Samy invested over a million dollars to build the restaurant in 2006 in order to fulfil Amy's dreams. About two years prior to the episode's filming, bloggers began writing negative reviews of the restaurant's food and the owners' 'bizarre' behaviours. Amy says the reviews were "lies" and states that they cost the restaurant a "tremendous amount of business".

The day before Ramsay arrives, the camera crew witnesses an intense argument between Samy and a customer. It starts when the customer complains to Samy that he and his friend has been waiting for a pizza for over an hour, causing Samy to lash out at him and order the two customers to leave, but not before insisting that the two customers pay for the drinks they have received. Samy then turns his attention to the customer's friend, while Amy threatens to call the police. Just when it appears that Samy and the customer will come to blows, a cameraman steps in and escorts the customers out of the restaurant. Amy then berates and insults the other customers in the restaurant before storming back into the kitchen.

Upon his arrival, Ramsay is initially impressed with the kitchen's good hygiene and organisation, though becomes more wary when Amy admits that she closes the restaurant if either she or Samy are not there. After the initial discussion, Ramsay prepares to sample the dishes. Though he liked one of the desserts he tried when meeting the couple initially, he had a rather negative response towards the other menu items: a fig and pear prosciutto pizza that was very sweet and made with under-cooked dough; the blue ribbon burger was not medium rare as requested, with a combination of condiments that Ramsay finds bizarre, and a bun dripping with grease; a red pepper ravioli that exhibits a combination of sweet and spicy flavours that Ramsay calls "confusing" and then he learns from Samy that it was mass-produced frozen ravioli despite the menu advertising it as freshly made; and a salmon burger that was overcooked and the presentation of it was unappealing. Samy reveals to Ramsay that he does not tell Amy about the problems with the dishes as he knows she does not deal well with criticism. (Know anyone like that?)

At one point during the sampling, Ramsay learns from one of the waitresses, that neither she nor the other servers make any tips, but that they instead go to Samy, on elf the owners. Ramsay discusses this with Samy, who justifies the policy by saying he does much of the front-of-house work; though Miranda reveals Samy does not always properly input the orders and often omits dishes that were ordered as a result of this.

As the episode progresses, we see that during dinner service, Ramsay criticises Amy and Samy for the food he was served during lunch and Amy responds by denying any wrongdoing because Samy refused to tell her the problems about the food. He also criticises her for using frozen ravioli instead of making it fresh, and announces to the customers, (which he was very famous for), that the ravioli is off the menu, which doesn't sit well with Amy. (But it makes good TV, wether you agree or not.) Throughout the night, customers are seen complaining about the long waiting, and several customers are shown sending back their dishes they disliked. At one point, Amy accidentally gives the wrong table number to a server. Subsequently, when giving food to another server, as well as the table number, Katy, (a waitress), asks "Are you sure?"

Amy responds by accusing her of having an "attitude problem" and demands that she should leave. When Ramsay witnesses a customer giving a tip intended for the servers and Samy taking it for himself, Samy again defends the policy, stating that the waiting staff receive an hourly wage. This prompts Ramsay to inform the customer that all tips go to the restaurant's management and not the servers, to which the customer replies, "That's horrible."

Samy and Ramsay then get into a heated, sweary argument, in which Ramsay tells Samy he is not allowed to take his servers' tips. Amy closes the restaurant, and fires Katy on the spot. Samy attempts to change Amy's mind, but Amy does not relent, later describing Katy, who leaves the premises in tears, as a "poisonous little viper".

Ramsay returns to the restaurant the next day, only to find it closed. Ramsay takes this time opportunity to talk to Henry and Jessica who previously worked in the restaurant. Both describe horrible working experiences; Henry claims Samy made him wash his car and Jessica claims that at least 50 people were fired during the 18-month period when she worked at the restaurant.

Ramsay then attempts to talk to Amy and Samy, telling them what they are doing wrong. Amy refuses to listen and becomes increasingly aggressive and hostile towards Ramsay. Samy even reveals that they had actually fired 100 employees, not 50. As a result, Ramsay realises they are not open to making any changes and leaves the restaurant, and in a concluding monologue, states that this is the first time he has met two restaurant owners that he could not help. He also started to talk to Pam, another worker, who admitted to Ramsay that on one occasion, Samy had hit her. Before leaving the area he cites the fact that the restaurant has gone through a hundred staff members, stating that Amy and Samy have upset the local community and are incapable of accepting criticism, and believes that they would not have adhered to any changes he would have implemented to improve the restaurant anyway

After the show aired, the restaurant, which is located in a shopping centre became a momentary tourist attraction. A plus you may say. Wrong. The restaurant received extensive negative feedback on their official Facebook page. When the owners Amy and Samy responded by denouncing people who posted negative comments, it provoked more of the same, not only on Facebook, but also on Yelp and Reddit. Forbes used the reactions as a 'poster example' of how a business should not react to comments on social media. The owners later stated that they were 'hacked', and that they had not posted any of the comments. This prompted more negative responses and the original comments and responses were eventually removed. As a result of the Kitchen Nightmares episode and Facebook posts, awareness of the incident caused the "meltdown" to go viral.

The company hired a local public relations firm, and a second Facebook page was eventually taken down as well, while another one called "I support Amy's Baking Company Bakery Boutique & Bistro 100 percent". A press release announced that they would be holding a "Grand Re-Opening" in May 2013. In April 2014, Kitchen Nightmares aired a special episode revolving around the events at Amy's Baking Company during and after the episode aired with a new, specially-recorded interview with the owners conducted by local reporter Ana Garcia. Amy's Baking Company permanently closed in September 2015. Amy Bouzaglo explained that the development stemmed from problems with the building's former landlord, and not the TV series. She also indicated her future career plans included making desserts for a Phoenix-area restaurant group and producing online instructional cooking videos. No-one cares what she does now.

You may think this is my favourite episode of the show. And you'd be right. But like I said, the lesson is that airing your laundry in public isn't great and although the show was edited for maximum effect I'm sure, what it did do was destroy a failing business. Then there are those that think Ramsay and the crew were also at fault. So like I said, no-one really comes out of this very well.

Baker didn't. Grade didn't. Jonathan Nathan-Turner didn't. The franchise didn't.

JNT believed that he was set to do other projects. The management didn't. So here we are at the end of 1986, with no lead, no script editor, no stories and a producer that had their hopes crushed with only four months to go until production started of a new series.

When news had got out of Baker's sacking, the production office was deluged with agents contacting them making suggestions for lead actors and a new face for the franchise. This was at odds with what happening with how the show was perceived by the public. Actors still thought it would look good on their CV, (maybe in the same way 'The Bill' and 'Casualty' did in the 90's and early 2000's), but the audience was switching off in droves.

Unlike the casting of the sixth Doctor where the producer was given free reign, JNT was ordered to do screen tests and auditions. For his part JNT told the press he was looking for a true eccentric, a polar opposite of the previous incarnation. Sylvester McCoy was recommended by another producer and by his agent, for being very eccentric and an excellent actor. He was often seen on stage with his head on fire, being punched, putting ferrets down his trousers or using a hammer to put nails up his nose. He went on to do some children's TV work including being a presenter on anarchic Saturday morning TV show 'Tiswas' alongside Chris Tarrant, Sally James, Lenny

Henry and Frank Carson. There were still doubts and he was auditioned and screen tested, which proved amongst those that were short listed, he was head and shoulders above the rest for the role.

A press conference was called where photo's of McCoy were taken of him in his everyday clothes with the TARDIS and the retained services of Bonnie Langford as his companion. The press chose to focus on the fact that McCoy was a relative unknown and were very lukewarm and very underwhelmed by the choice. Perhaps the publics interest had peaked with the 20th Anniversary and it was also noted that the interest was beginning to more than wain. Many pointing to poor stories, poor effects and losing touch with what the public actually wanted.

As relaunches were going, this was going to be tough. Our next lesson is the determination that it takes to 'whip up' excitement in today's world there is constant 'noise'. Ironically with the social media platforms of today, we have never been more connected, but never been more disconnected. That's because there is TOO much noise. Everyone is their own media outlet, talking, posting, videoing, snap chatting, tweeting and shouting…all at the same time. As it stands in the world today, there is no such thing as an overnight success. To get something 'noticed' it could be weeks, months and even years.

Take the case of UK videographer Phil Beastall. At the start of the December, a tradition has started where for some reason or another, people are eager to see Department Store, John Lewis's Christmas advert. It's premiere is usually an advert that is 3 to 4 minutes long that tells a story. In previous years it's been about the man on the moon or a monster under a child's bed. This year however, was a story of how Elton John became who he is today, by the gift of a piano on Christmas Day. Personally, it left me a little underwhelmed as all I saw it as a blatant plug for his biopic that comes out in 2019. Then a video began to be shared all around the internet of a young man, who was counting down to Christmas. It had some very emotional music and was done very much in the style of a John Lewis Christmas Advert Story. The video ends with the man sat at his kitchen table listening to a Walkman and putting in a cassette to listen to the voice of his mother. His deceased mother. I defy anyone to watch it and not feel slightly emotional.

I was very fortunate to have interviewed Phil for my 'Your Best Kept Business Secret' podcast to talk to him about it. It had been a wild few weeks as the video, on show over several internet media platforms, had been viewed more than 16 million times. The beauty of it? The video cost £50 to make. My point of this story here? It had been filmed 2 years prior to when it 'took off' and caught interest. Hardly an 'overnight success', but shows you that sometimes to catch your customers or clients imagination you have to promote and share something that is relevant to your ideal market. I wonder how much money John Lewis could have saved with Phil Beastall and not Elton John.

The relaunch got even worse. Without Baker, the show required the Doctor to regenerate at the start of the episode as opposed to the end as per previous incarnations. The fact that budget and production wouldn't allow the show to use old footage of Baker, the writers concocted a situation where the TARDIS crashes onto a planet and as the enemies board it, turn an unconscious Doctor over on to his back, where it's revealed, even through some TV trickery, McCoy in a blonde curly-haired wig regenerating into himself. Comical is a word I'd use here.

However McCoy was actually a good fit for the role, even if the timing sucked. He used the eccentricities of famous intellectuals, along with the cosmic hobo look of the second Doctor. As spoken of earlier, things tend to go round in cycles and new script editor Andrew Cartmel wanted to take the show into a darker direction, with more social commentaries rather than the light entertainment flavour that JNT had doused it in whenever he could. However his employment so late in the day, meant that he had limited opportunity to influence the first season of the McCoy era. These ideas tended to permeate the last two seasons and therefore this era can be viewed almost as a tale of two parts. The more light entertainment on one hand and the darker, good story telling part on the other.

And here comes the next lesson. McCoy's first season was inconsistent to say the least. It's tone and quality often changed, sometimes mid-episode, but it was because of several factors. It's rushed production, restrictive budget, and because of prior interference from above was becoming schizophrenic trying to please the general public, the fans of yesteryear and moral crusaders that wanted the violence toned and watered down. It was trying to do too many things for too many people. In business the safest thing to do is to know exactly who you're trying to please and how. Even more important is that whilst perfection is just time wasted, a customer, client or public have a certain expectation of a minimum product or service they are putting in. So if if something isn't ready, rushed or inconsistent, it will become quickly obvious. It's at this point that customers or clients have a decision to make. Stick with you or find another provider for the same product or service that is consistent. Remember the story about the hare and the tortoise? Yup…as old as the hills, but is right every freaking time.

One of the other problems with series was the Doctors companion Mel Bush, played by 'Pantomime Queen' Bonnie Langford. The character was very underwritten and became quite an annoyance with her screams at the end of the episodes matching the pitch of the sting of the theme music! (Quite a talent to be fair!) Andrew Cartmell, the script editor was very aware that she wouldn't fit in with the vision of the show and at the end of the first season was pretty much unceremoniously dumped from the series and replaced within seconds..I kid you not…by a polar opposite in the the tomboy character of ACE.

Onto the second season and the Seventh Doctor developed into a much darker figure than any of his earlier incarnations, manipulating people like chess pieces and always seeming to be playing a deeper game. A distinguishing feature of McCoy's performances was his manner of speech. He used his natural slight Scottish accent and rolled his r's. But a lesson to be learned from a series of episodes that marked it's 25th year should encourage business owners. There is the saying that states, "There is no such thing as a new idea." And they're right, but in the story was called 'Remembrance of the Daleks', the franchise marked a change of something classic. But at the same time it also marked the change of a classic that was of added value and would be still around to this day. In this case, non-fans, (and some fans) of the show always used to laugh that the best way to get away from a Dalek was to go upstairs, because they couldn't. Until now.

One of the cliff-hangers to the episodes was the Doctor being locked in a basement as a Dalek chased him. We're left with the image of the Dalek hovering above the steps moving closer to the Doctor. A simple idea, but an effective one and some 17 years before the new series (After 2005-) really got to use it.  So adding something of real value, that can be used to a classic product or service is an excellent way of renewing it, selling more of it or making more money from it.

The age old issue of scheduling reared it's ugly head again. And this one shows how some decisions just can't be explained. The show was scheduled on a Wednesday evening versus the long-running soap opera, Coronation Street. It was decision, and I can't believe I'm about to write this, that was based on the stupid assumption that as a human you can't be a fan of both shows. Seriously. Not every house had video recorders and it wasn't quite in our psyche yet to record and go back and watch it maybe a day or two later. The viewing figures dropped like a stone to an average of less than 5.5 million. It was not recovering the viewers it had lost in the hiatus and more bad news was to come as the promotional budget in which the franchise was to run to was depleted again due to several production costs rising and so McCoy's last series launched with about as much fanfare as a trumpet in the middle of the arctic circle. It launched opposite Coronation Street and a World Cup Qualifying match, televised by it's own corporation on BBC2. (A channel that showed repeats, documentaries and Open University programming.)

It was a staggering decision and showed how little bosses not only viewed the franchise, but it's fans and effectively a paying public. You could argue that with decisions like this you could have one of two trains of thought. The powers that be were either utterly incompetent or they really did want to kill the franchise. The first episode bought in only 3.1 million viewers…a rating so low it gets the award for the lowest EVER rating for an episode of Dr Who, in any era.

Sometimes market conditions don't allow you to do certain things at certain times. I know..I know..I've already said that perfection is just time wasted and there is no such thing as a perfect time. However through this example of incompetence or management malice, it goes to show that sometimes you are better holding your powder dry, and waiting for a better opportunity to go with something. It's a bit like launching a brand new Christmas Pudding on Easter Sunday. Or a revolutionary heath treatment on April 1st. It's just not credible that it would work. In this situation, the odds were firmly stacked against it. Could the franchise have survived if it had been relaunched on a different day opposite two different shows? Maybe. But in this case the 'goodwill' with the public had deteriorated to a point that people rightly or wrongly just didn't care anymore.

Whenever a new product our service is launched there should always be a consideration put to the marketing budget. It's something that many small business owners just don't do. They start something or open something and then think that people will find them. No. Doesn't work that way. Whatever budget you have in business, the more you put into good marketing, the greater the chance you have of reaching more ideal customers and clients. It's one thing that bothers me with many business owners is that they spend way too much time looking at the bottom figure in their business and that's the one of the money coming in. If as a business you spend more time and money increasing the pool in which you mix with your customers and clients, the bottom figure of money coming in will look after itself. In fact it's likely to increase.

**Chief Caretaker**: I am the chief caretaker.

**The Doctor**: And I am —

**Chief Caretaker**: No need to tell me, I know who you are. We have been waiting for this momentous visit for so many years. You were the man who brought Paradise Towers to life, the visionary who dreamed up its pools and lifts and squares, and now you have returned to your creation. You will make all those dilapidated lifts rise and fall as they have never done before! All signs of wall-scrawl will disappear from the corridors of Paradise Towers! The floors will gleam, the windows will shine and all will be made as new! Fellow caretakers, you know who this is? This is the great architect, returned to Paradise Towers! Bid him welcome! All hail the great architect, all hail!

**Caretakers**: All hail the great architect!

**Caretaker**: What should we do with him now chief?

**Chief Caretaker**: *[beat]* Kill him.

Michael Grade left to go to Channel 4, and his successor, Jonathan Powell, (previous head of BBC1, who had already tried to bin the franchise once), harboured a dim view of Dr Who and an even dimmer view of it's producer John Nathan-Turner. In one interview he was quoted as saying, "I just wanted him to f@@@ off and solve it…or die really. But it had probably gone beyond solving. The only way of resuscitating it was to put a new producer on it…but we didn't want to resuscitate it." After the disappointing launch of the new series and having not let JNT move on, on several occasions, Powell sensed his chance to do what Grade had failed to do.

Arguably by the end of 1989, the franchise, story wise was very much back on track. Story arcs, quality acting and thought provoking themes were all in place, but it had run out steam from the publicity it received back in 1985 when Grade and Powell had tried to take it off our screens then. So Powell showed no restraints in doing what he felt he needed to do any longer. With a mist, (not a fog), of vague assurances it may come back, an independent production company and some sizeable foreign (American) investment, Dr Who was quietly killed off. A franchise running 26 years, suffocated by people who treated it with little or no respect…seeing no further than the end of their noses. In one of those bizarre twist of fate, Sylvester McCoy recorded his last speech as the Doctor on Thursday 23rd November 1989, exactly 26 years to the day that the show first aired. It was very understated, but to the serious fans of the franchise it left people with that feeling that although it had been killed off, the name would always be out there, in peoples minds and imaginations and one day would return.

The lesson here is the legacy that you leave behind. And by legacy in business perhaps I don't mean the things that someone like Steve jobs has left us. Or that Bill Gates and Elon Musk will leave behind. I mean what do people say about you when you're not in the room? What do you want them to say about you when you're no longer here? Many brands and franchises have gone under either dying a slow and quiet death or a loud public one, but sometimes those brands can be revived in a slightly different format. Woolworths went online. Toys R Us now lives on in Asia and surrounding countries.

"There are worlds out there where the sky is burning, and the sea's asleep, and the rivers dream; people made of smoke and cities made of song. Somewhere there's danger, somewhere there's injustice, and somewhere else the tea's getting cold. Come on, Ace. We've got work to do."

We know that Dr Who lived on to fight another day, but it was going to be a long wait for that to happen…

So here are the lessons we learned from the seventh Doctors era:

1. **It doesn't matter what someone does to you, the smartest and wisest thing to do is not to 'air your laundry' in public**. No-one ever comes out of it well and it's way too easy to do. With people looking for things to 'parade' some years

later than they were published or written, businesses and their owners need to be more conscious than ever of being respectful to their customers, competitors or fans.

2. **Don't expect to make a noise the first time, the second or even the third time**. There is no such thing as an overnight success and to be frank with you, you don't need to be either. For some overnight success is two years, for others like KFC founder, Colonel Sanders it could be as long as 65 years. Just keep creating hype and opportunities to get noticed.

3. **Take your time to get it right and consistent**. Notice I didn't say 'perfect', because it's just time wasted. If it's of good quality and you deliver the product or service at a regularly high level, then do it. Rushing and doing things in half measures or cutting corners should never be an option for a business or it's owners.

4. **Update existing products and service with added value**. You don't have to re-invent the wheel, just add value to it. Can it be smaller, bigger, faster, more precise, easier to use or better designed? It can be the simplest of things that can update a product or service that can make it look or seem new to clients and customers. It can also make it more valuable to them and therefore willing to pay more or purchase more often.

5. **Know when you're going to be beaten**. If market conditions aren't right, then keep your powder dry. Wait for a more opportune time than when competition is tough. Pivot what you're doing ever so slightly, so you're not operating in the same space as others that maybe bigger or more popular. And never launch a new product or service on April 1st...do I really need to tell you why?

6. **Marketing is the most important thing in a budget**. Don't keep looking at the money coming in because if you take your eye off the top of the funnel, ie getting people into your sales stream you will find that those numbers you've been staring at will begin to get smaller or standstill. Keep a focus at the top and the rest will usually take care of itself.

7. **Think hard**. What do you want your legacy to be? What do you want your customers and clients to say about you when you are no longer around? Can your brand live on and what will it be remembered for?

It would be 7 years before we saw the Doctor again and would it be worth the wait..?

# The Eighth Doctor

With the Doctor pitted against the hit TV soap Coronation Street, it's effects stuck in the time warp of the 1960's theatre and everyone on the production wanting it to be 'better' and no-one willing to put any money into it, it's cancellation was inevitable. It would take 7 years for someone to bring the brand back and no one episode, no series or movie had so much trouble getting to screen as that of Paul McGann's version of the Doctor.

There was no-one in house to bring it back. It was hated by many on the executive floors and should be classed as a 'taboo project'. No-one willing to put their name forward, but interestingly there were several approaches from outside of the corporation to make a feature film. Step forward Philip Segal. After emigrating to the USA in his early teens, Segal had pursued a career in American TV and by the 1990's was working on Drama Development for Columbia Pictures Television in Los Angeles. He was a fan of the series and it took some convincing of his other executives that a Dr Who series maybe an interesting path to go down. He made some initial enquiries with the BBC, first touching base with the commercial arm, BBC Enterprises.

He first approached the BBC mere weeks before the corporation decided to give the series a 'long rest'. Did the enquiry contribute to the cancellation or was the timing mere coincidence? We'll never know. But there was no love for the project at the corporation and it was the dawn of independent TV production.

Here's the first lesson from this Doctor. As a business owner trying to do things on your own is always difficult. Cheap, yes. But difficult. Some of you may have heard of affiliate marketing and this is becoming more and more common place in today's business world. It's where a business has your audience and they promote your products or services for a cut of the return you get. It kind of makes sense. You are being validated by the audience owner who is happy to share your products and services to their customers. It makes it easier to get your message out to others and can help you grow your business and customer base. In this case reaching out to someone within the BBC helped Segal get meetings and 'airtime' and you'll see how important it is as we continue through the chapter.

There was no love for the project anymore on the executive floors of the BBC and they certainly, at that time, didn't want to be associated with anything that in their opinion should have been put to sleep years ago. In early 1989, the BBC announced that it wouldn't entertain anymore discussion on a co-produced TV series as a company called Coast to Coast had stumped up £750k for the rights to produce a theatrical movie release of Dr Who. For the BBC, it seemed it was a movie or nothing at all.

I guess here is the next lesson. If you value something and want to 'do something' with a name or a 'brand', just do it. Later on you'll see what a waste of £750k this actually was, but names like Woolworths and even Toys R Us live on in a different guise in the form of online stores now rather than bricks and mortar shops. There is something saddening about me writing this as I remember both of those brands very fondly from my childhood, but it is nice that things live on when life changes. Dr Who did this after this TV Movie. It lived on in audio play format, where no one never needed to worry about what the special effects looked like. It became big business for the company that bought the licence, BIG Finish. Reviving other well known TV and SciFi series has also become a home run for the company. Sapphire and Steel, The Avengers, Terrahawks and Stargate are just some of the licences that the company now use and even though the programmes they're based on have stopped production. Each one can sound new and fresh, because we have to use our imagination. The actors are as we remember them. Lovingly crafted and produced with pride, they are the TV shows you wanted to see but couldn't because of the time, the budgets or simply the lack of imagination in the writing.

In 1991, with the potential movie gathering hype with actors such as Donald Sutherland linked to playing the Timelord, Segal moved to the TV Production arm of Amblin Entertainment. This would prove important to the BBC as Amblin Entertainment was owned by the most famous movie director in the world at the time...a certain Steven Spielberg. It was the finest calling card he ever get.

This is where the lesson of credibility comes in. There is a question that I'm often asked, which is "How can I get credibility?" Well my friend there is no hard and fast rule to this, it's a mixture of things. As I write this book I've been lucky enough to have been involved with the BBC in both radio and television. I haven't had my own show, but I have been asked for interviews on what's happening in business. I've also been fortunate enough to be asked to speak on business subjects by companies such as Hitachi, Mercedes Benz and Siemens. I've also been fortunate enough to speak in front of a crowd of 6 people at a local networking event. It's fair to say that perhaps that lat one is not on the front of my website, but it was AS valuable to me doing that as it is speaking to hundreds of people.

My point here is that I had to put myself in front of the right people to get these credibility points. For Hitachi I became best friends with , (and eventually partner of), the Marketing Manager. I invited them to an event that I was running for free. For Siemens, a friend of mine double booked themselves, so I rearranged MY diary to take up the opportunity with less than 48hrs notice. If the BBC rang and said can you get in your car and drive up the M6 to be on BBC Breakfast at 6:55am tomorrow morning? I would rescheduled a few things, go to bed early and set off at 4am the next morning. If I hear a debate on the radio and strongly oppose what the guest is saying, I'll ring up, text in or email the show telling them that their expert is an idiot.

You have to look to what kind of credibility you really want. Is it working with big brands or companies or is it the case studies that you can put forward to your public about how you turned someone's life or business around? Sometimes this means doing stuff for free. Especially if you're a start-up. I'm not saying go overboard and make yourself broke, but what I am saying is that if you can specially select a few people or businesses that have some 'weight' in the industry or niche that you're in, then the credibility will go miles and miles. It takes work. You must always be looking for opportunities to gain credibility. What's happening in the news? What's happening in your industry that people should be talking about? Think of yourself as a 'go-to expert' in your field. Grab the opportunity to be the top of the speed dial list when a National News story breaks and its about your field of work or business. And if it's not happening, MAKE it happen. Rearrange meetings and phone calls, just so you can grow your credibility. It goes a long, long, long way. And can last a long, long time. Short term pain for longer term gain.

Believe it or not Spielberg was actually interested in the Dr Who project, and he gave Segal his blessing to go after it. However the BBC decided that it needed 'more of a rest'. The BBC hated it and the thought of putting any resources behind it, was just a no go. It had been an embarrassing failure in it's last 5 years of transmission. But down at BBC Enterprises, (soon to become BBC Worldwide) it was a different story. It was making them a lot of money, but the Corporation and Enterprises just never worked in tandem and were definitely singing from different hymn sheets. BBC Enterprises could see there was still some love for the Timelord, because they were the arm of the BBC that made and marketed the video's.

Yet there was someone else who 'liked it'. A certain Alan Yentob, controller of BBC2 from 1987. Yentob had bought Star Trek: The Next Generation to BBC2 in an early evening time-slot and he certainly saw the appeal of sci-fi. He had been corresponded to about the show on a daily basis by die-hard Dr Who fans. He didn't see it as trash, but oddly something to be proud of. So he called for re-runs of Dr Who in that same slot in 1992. And ratings wise, for that time and on that channel it quickly became successful.

In 1993, Yentob took over as controller of BBC1 and because of him showing the re-runs, rumour and counter rumour suggested that the Doctor maybe on his way back. Meanwhile BBC Enterprises came forward with their own ambitious plan for the Timelord with a 30th Anniversary Special Feature Film, only to be released on video. But Coast to Coast still had the rights to the Dr Who Movie. With merely 30 days left of this, and they had to be in physical production of a movie for them to retain them. Their scheme was to hire Star Trek legend, Leonard Nimoy to film a couple of weeks of second unit. This would then trigger an extension of the agreement and lock up the rights for years to come. Segal spoke to Nimoy and told him what they were trying to do and he got cold feet and ran away from the project.

By chance Yentob was at the Amblin lott in the US and requested a tour of the sets of Segal's programme SeaQuest DSV. Usually he would have assigned someone to do this but on hearing that Yentob was one of the BBC party, Segal thought this was too big a chance to pass up to tell him his vision of the new Dr Who. He took him to one side and lobbied him, driving him crazy. Fortuitously Spielberg turned up on set and was introduced to Yentob, with talk of the Director being involved in Dr Who in the same breath. That there...that was credibility.

By now the BBC were taking the Amblin deal seriously. Who wouldn't? Steven Spielberg for crying out loud! Segal began to to try to make a co-production deal and it took so much time. It dragged on and on. Lawyers were involved and Segal began to hound them on both sides as he felt they were just trying to kill the deal. He became obsessed, and the more people said 'no', the harder he pushed. The prospect of the show coming back was leaked to the media and Steven Spielberg's name was now being dragged into it. It became apparent that the only way this was going to happen was by having a 'friend' inside the BBC, so step forward Tony Greenwood of BBC Worldwide Television and he became a close ally. He would literally speak to Segal and walk down the corridor to speak to Yentob himself. It was the only way stuff was going to get done.

The next lesson is the art of 'Getting S***t Done!'. Way too many people just give up after a few knock backs. The amount of sales people who waste their day because the first few calls they made said 'no'. That's THEIR fault that they are not earning the money they should be. It's their fault if they take it easy and give up because someone said 'no'. Segal to his credit became more and more tenacious. Not desperate. People can smell desperate a bloody mile off. Getting your hands dirty and working hard makes you lucky. But there is no such thing as 'luck' in business. The harder you work, the 'luckier' you get, simple. Segal wasn't getting lucky, he was grabbing as many opportunities and pissing as many people off as he needed to do, to get the opportunity that he had set his heart on.

The BBC and Segal came to an understanding and commissioned a 'Bible' of what the story would be, why the show was back, why it would be different along with schedules and budgets. New CGI animations of the Daleks and Dr Who 'Bible' were then created. Now that left the question about who was going to play the Doctor. Actors linked with the role were Robert Lindsay, Eric Idol, Tim Curry, Billy Connolly, Jonathan Pryce and Trevor Eve. But Segal wanted Michael Crawford or Michael Palin. Crawford felt he was too old and Palin didn't think he could do the character justice. Segal was introduced to the movie 'Withnail and I', and the choice was made for Paul McGann.

But there was yet another stumbling block. The drafted, redrafted and re-redrafted script didn't make Spielberg happy. It showed no unique way at looking at the 30 year old Timelord or his story. And despite Spielberg's involvement Segal was also struggling to find a network willing to show the production. Salvation came in the form of Trevor Walton a British born Executive at the FOX TV Networks, TV Movie Division. He'd understood that Segal was in possession of Dr Who and if he couldn't set it up as a series, he requested he see him first for a potential TV Movie. It wasn't about hearing a pitch. It wasn't about being curious as to what was happening. He wanted to make it. Full stop.

I guess Segal's 'luck' was starting pay off.

They met in his office. Talked nostalgically about Dr Who for twenty minutes and then Walton simply said, "That's great...let's get going." Later that afternoon Segal called him to make sure..."Is this a script commitment or are we making a movie?" "We're making a movie." Replied Walton.

Dr Who was BACK!

But there was yet another problem. The BBC and Amblin had been in discussion about a continuing series and not a TV movie. To the BBC it felt a bit naff. Which was odd considering the lack of love, care and attention it had received towards the end of it's run. Segal made the decision to try use the TV Movie as a 'back-door pilot'. The movie wasn't ideal but at least it could happen. It was going to be made.

The first script was terrible and was dismissed out of hand. At that same time, Spielberg wanted his name and his company name taken off the project. He wanted nothing to do with it. So as they began pre-production the BBC weren't even aware that Amblin were no longer a partner in the project. Segal kept this quiet until the deal was too far down the road to do anything about it. I guess there should be a piece about 'sharp practice' here so it would be remiss of me to not to talk about it.

Segal's tactics here perhaps should not be followed in business terms. It was a plain piece of mis-information and could easily have bought about the collapse of the project. Think about in personal terms. A friend tells you a little white lie so as not to worry you. But because they are worried you might spot the lie, another lie is tagged on to it. Which makes it a bigger lie. And then another lie is developed to stop you spotting the two lies that you've already made and then it begins to run out of control. Look, here's a fact about business and life.

We all f*** up sometimes. All of us. Admit it, deal with it and move on. Some of the most successful people in the world have been bankrupt. They f***ed up. Admitted it and got on with the job of not repeating the same mistakes again. If you don't it continues to run the risk of mistrust and your business relationships will never be the same again, if at all. Remember there are other 'you's' out there doing the same thing as you. Be honest. If something isn't as it should be, admit it, deal with it and get on with not doing it again.

A new writer was bought in as an effort to keep Spielberg and Amblin on board. The new script was just as bad, with a comical side-kick called Lizzy and her Bulldog called 'Winston', (nothing like a good stereo type is there?) At the exact same time, Segal was offered a position at Paramount as an independent producer. He took it.

Writer Matthew Jacobs was bought in to draft a completely new story and new script. It was a smart move. The script bought back an old Doctor at the start of this story, much to the delight of fans and at odds with the BBC. They weren't happy with the idea of having Sylvester McCoy at the start of the TV Movie. To them, this was a nod to the fact that the show hadn't finished on a high and with who they considered a very unpopular Doctor. (Time will argue otherwise) Remember this was to have a 'life' in the US as well as the UK and it didn't make sense to the

British side of the project that this incarnation of the franchise should be related to something that had become an embarrassing joke in the eyes of the public and TV Executives. But Segal wanted to connect the show to it's roots and it's strong fan base. On them he could rely.

There is that ridiculous saying, 'Too Many Cooks Spoil the Broth'. Firstly I've had some awful tasting broth cooked by one cook and secondly I would argue that a lot of cooks could make the kitchen more productive and allow for differing variations. But there were so many people trying to give the script writer notes and ideas and in his own words, "The trick is to keep your head when everyone around you is losing theirs...". Yes they were worried about sinking millions into this project but it was almost an impossible task to keep everyone happy. There was BBC TV, BBC Worldwide, Amblin, Universal and FOX all with an opinion and different interests.

The problem in this project and any business project is when the ideas just don't marry up. Not one set of notes matched another. Too many fingers in the project pie. Segal couldn't please everyone and tried to make the best of what he had. He took many of the BBC's notes and the networks, but ignored everyone else's. Effectively what we got instead of the blockbuster that Segal had visioned was a hotchpotch of ideas and instead of a fine broth, we ended up getting a muddy stew instead.

Geoffrey Sax was quickly given the role of Director, and he accepted partly because he was promised a 30 Day shoot rather than a usual 20 day shoot on TV movies. Daphne Ashbrook was cast as the Doctors assistant, but there were always going to be trade-off's and the Master was to be an American star...although we got Eric Roberts, Julia's less famous brother. The commercialism took over where finding someone who would have been right for the role would have been better. In fairness Eric wasn't that bad, but it was a bit of a square peg in a well rounded hole.

So the lesson is here that if you sacrifice creativity for fame and fortune, perhaps the end result isn't going to be as good as you hoped. Sometimes it does pay off, but in very few cases. If you want something and believe in it that passionately, then you have to decide wether the trade off is worth it. If you want a Picasso and end up with a Citroen car then you can only blame yourself. If you want a Picasso you either wait and save the money to get one or learn how to paint one yourself. The satisfaction in getting a Picasso and being able to admire it and stare at it far outweighs any short term satisfaction from looking at a postcard or driving a rather odd shaped Citroen car. So if you believe in it keep it. If you compromise, you probably didn't hold that belief that highly anyway.

The projects budget started to get eaten away. The Canadian dollar was getting stronger and Universal started to renege on earlier financial commitments, so this meant that shooting days were reducing. Add to that the ending of the script still was being written and rewritten. No one was quite satisfied with anything. Segal felt he was stuck in the middle and being a referee rather than given creative leadership. The writer himself says that of the finished movie he was only happy with 60% to 70% and at the point of the Millenium Clock, the whole thing began to unravel as he was trying to please too many people. He felt he got the character right, but there were just too many vested interests.

When it arrived on the screens in the UK, ratings wise it did really well. Lots of publicity and was a bit of a TV event. But in the US where they hoped it would do well it was scheduled up against the (then) last ever Rosanne show and did poorly. Segal was forced to bin his ideas of a new series. Although it didn't do as well as hoped, it did bring the Doctor back into to peoples minds and showed there was still an appetite for the continuing stories of the Timelord.

If you go back and watch the TV Movie again, it actually holds up quite well and yes, you can perhaps see why it didn't go on to be a series. The highlight of the project was Paul McGann. He became the Doctor and thankfully he kept the franchise going in it's continued 'wilderness' years through the audio dramas produced by BIG Finish. He did get to make one more appearance as the Timelord for the 50th anniversary special. In a short piece written by Stephen Moffat, he materialised aboard a space craft that was about to crash. He then regenerated into the 'War Doctor' and got the regeneration that ever actor who plays the role should get.

For Segal this project was a highlight in his career and about getting something done after 7 years. It was a passion project and if you have the passion and the drive you CAN get something done. Don't ever give up...they will come true.

So here are the lessons from the 8th Doctor...

1. **Doing things on your own is difficult**. I get it...being a business owner is a proud thing, but don't let your pride get in the way of success. If there is someone out there willing to help you get in front of your audience, let them help! It can also be a great source of income generation for you. Give them a cut, and don't expect any help for free. You are just getting in your own way if you don't reach out.
2. **If you have something of worth, do something with it**. We're seeing more and more brands

come alive elsewhere rather than the bricks and mortar they used to be housed in. Don't let something good and great sit on the shelves gathering dust...you could be sat on a money spinner if you do it right.

3. **Take any and every opportunity to build your credibility**. It won't just appear. If the TV or Radio wants to interview you, rearrange your schedule to do it. If you haven't got any connections in the media yet, go get some. If there are opportunities to work with businesses that you want to, take them. Get into positions where they want to talk to you and want to hear what you have to say. Use every opportunity to speak and be on a stage. Your credibility is your calling card.

4. **Get S### Done**. If you are passionate about achieving a goal...get on with it. Otherwise you're just another day, week, month or year away from achieving what you wanted. And in business there is a massive danger that if you stand still long enough you'll get run over and someone else will overtake you. So badger, hustle (hate that word), persevere and 'Get S### Done'.

5. Perhaps this should have been after #3, but please **don't mis-represent yourself**. You will get found out eventually. It's very easy to hide things or not tell people things, but when the truth surfaces and it will, it's very, very difficult to get that trust back. If you've f###ed up. Admit it. Deal with it. Get on with it.

6. **There may well be compromises** along the way, but if it's a value that you hold dear, then you shouldn't compromise. On the flip side you'll have to be prepared to walk away and leave a deal or some business on the table if you don't want to compromise. Fact of business life I'm afraid.

7. **If you want something so badly, be prepared to work for it.** There will be high points and there will probably be many, many more low points. If you want it...it's yours. If you give up...you probably never really wanted it badly enough in the first place.

And now I can hear the 'Cloister Bells'...it appears I have one more trip in me and then it's over to the next one...But I want to say something before I go...

# Before I Go...

"A straight line maybe the shortest distance between two points, but it is by no means the most interesting."

The Doctor

So my faithful companion we've made it to the end. And I hope I've opened your eyes to a few ideas in the business universe from a universe that was pretty much made out of cardboard, wood, bubble wrap and sticky tape.

It's amazing if you think about it that the franchise lasted to the point where we finish. But it does show you a MASSIVE learning that I'll come to at the end.

Here are the things we've talked about..

1. Opportunity
2. Test stuff
3. Graft
4. Give people a reason 'why'
5. View your competitors as a nemesis
6. Recognise the time for change
7. No one wants to be the person who follows 'the guy', but inevitably it will happen
8. Being that person will divide opinion
9. When the next generation fails, it's not the end

10. Look at your business and the world around you in equal measure
11. Businesses should use emotions in selling and their positioning
12. Are you cutting your nose off to spite your face?
13. Knowing when to get out
14. Doing what you can within a budget is a 'Golden Rule in Business'
15. Moving away from core principles and values is a risk
16. If you diversify, make sure you're spinning the right plates
17. There are no such things as new ideas
18. If you look flash, make sure the product or service backs it up
19. Connect on a personal level with your customers
20. Backwards steps are sometimes needed to move forwards
21. If you were successful once, going back to something can be a risk
22. Colours and Logo's
23. Competition is inspiring
24. Ask for help
25. If you're going to be anything in business, it's be authentic
26. If you represent a business or a brand, you should always put them first
27. You aren't bigger than any business or any brand
28. Strong women rock. Fact.

29. Handing over the baton is always a good idea
30. Going back to the past is only where SOME of the answers are
31. Experiment with new things, but not to the detriment of the original product
32. Get everyone on the same page when changes happen
33. If you're going to employ someone or put someone in place to work with a team, make sure there is a connection between them
34. Is the line of management or decision makers within your business the right one
35. Substance over image
36. Manage peoples expectations and manage your own at the same time
37. We have exactly 7 seconds in which to make a good impression
38. Don't water stuff down just because of the cost implications
39. If you see someone in the business sabotaging the business, do something about it.
40. Yes have an opinion, but don't be afraid to change it
41. Ask the your customers
42. It doesn't matter what someone does to you, the smartest and wisest thing to do is not to 'air your laundry' in public
43. Don't expect to make a noise the first time, the second or even the third time
44. Take your time to get it right and consistent

45. Update existing products and service with added value
46. Know when you're going to be beaten
47. Marketing is the most important thing in a budget
48. Think hard
49. Doing things on your own is difficult
50. If you have something of worth, do something with it
51. Take any and every opportunity to build your credibility.
52. Get S### Done
53. Perhaps this should have been after #3, but please don't mis-represent yourself
54. There may well be compromises along the way, but if it's a value that you hold dear, then you shouldn't compromise
55. If you want something so badly, be prepared to work for it

The MASSIVE learning? There may well be Dr Who fans reading this, but I've always known the fandom to be called 'Whovians', so my apologies if you don't call yourself that. They have a passion and determination for the franchise that is probably only matched by the people who dress up in Star Wars or Star Trek clothing. But after all the years of crap they had to put up with, they were the ones that were prepared to run through brick walls for Dr Who. Restore it to some sort of glory and put it back on the TV screens of the world.

What would you do if you had a customer base like that? How quickly could your business grow and expand if your customers would talk about you in the same way the fans talked about 'their' show'. And that's the thing. This franchise was never the BBC's at the end of the day. It was the viewers show. It was the fans show. Their loyalty now rewarded with a show that has won awards, critical acclaim and continues to lead the way in TV circles.

This is true with the franchise and with business... "It's not about you. It just starts with you."

Remember that, and you'll go far.

And so I'll leave you with this...true in business and in life...

"There's a lot of things you need to get across the universe. Warp drive...wormhole refractors...but you know the thing you need most of all? You need a hand to hold."

Time to go Sarah-Jane. Time to go...

# References

My childhood
Wikipedia
YouTube
Radio Free Skaro Podcast
Rory Sutherland, TedX, YourTube
Ramsay Kitchen Nightmares
The Billion Dollar Blowout
BBC News
Sky News
Austin Kleon, 'Show Your Work'

www.ingramcontent.com/pod-product-compliance
Lightning Source LLC
Chambersburg PA
CBHW071422180526
45170CB00001B/190